What your child needs from you
Creating a connected family

Justin Coulson, PhD

ACER Press

First published 2012
by ACER Press, an imprint of
Australian Council *for* Educational Research Ltd
19 Prospect Hill Road, Camberwell
Victoria, 3124, Australia

www.acerpress.com.au
sales@acer.edu.au

Edited by Elisa Webb
Cover design, text design and typesetting by ACER Project Publishing
Cover image © Tim Coulson Photography 2012

Printed in Australia by BPA Print Group

National Library of Australia Cataloguing-in-Publication entry:

Author:	Coulson, Justin.
Title:	What your child needs from you : creating a connected family / Justin Coulson.
ISBN:	9781742860435 (pbk.)
Notes:	Includes bibliographical references.
Subjects:	Parenting--Handbooks, manuals, etc. Child rearing--Handbooks, manuals, etc. Parent and child--Handbooks, manuals, etc. Discipline of children--Handbooks, manuals, etc.

Dewey Number: 649.1

This book is printed on carbon neutral paper derived from
well-managed forests and other controlled sources certified
against Forest Stewardship Council® standards, a non-profit
organisation devoted to encouraging the responsible
management of the world's forests.

For Nanna Bunt

'One of the most thoughtful, intelligent discussions of parenting. I found myself nodding my head in agreement, talking to friends and family about passages, and immediately applying techniques. A fantastic resource for the most difficult and meaningful part of our lives.'

Dr Todd B Kashdan

Professor of Psychology at George Mason University and author of Curious? Discover the Missing Ingredient to a Fulfilling Life and Designing Positive Psychology

'I just love the way this book is written – very practical, very focused on parent issues and at the same time very humble; Justin is not saying, "Do as I say because I'm the expert", but rather, "Here are some ideas that seem to work. What do you think?" It's practical, easy to read, well referenced and covers so many of the day-to-day topics that parents agonise about. It's also well presented in case studies, summary points, quotes ... and everything to make this book an eminently readable and sensible addition to any parent's library.'

Dr John Irvine

Child and Family Psychologist, Dr John's Happy Families Psychological Services

'Justin seems to have a sixth sense about parenting dilemmas, answering the questions that keep you up at night as well as illuminating the things that make family life meaningful. He manages to shine a light on those tricky issues and show you a path that fills you with resolve to be a better parent. Justin offers simple tools and frameworks that not only make you a better parent, but a happier one too.'

Alex Brooks

kidspot.com.au

'This is an important book on arguably the most important topic of all. Justin does a fantastic job of distilling the latest parenting research into readable and practical words of advice mums and dads so desperately want and need.'

Prof Timothy Sharp (Dr Happy)
Executive coach and consultant, facilitator and speaker

'We think parenting is about raising our kids. But as Justin so aptly points out, it is about raising ourselves. We need to become better people to raise our kids well, and Justin offers insight and advice on how to do just that: engage emotionally with your children, work with your children so they learn, and grab meaning wherever you can. This helps grow resilient kids and connected parents.'

Jodie Benveniste
Psychologist, parenting author and director of Parent Wellbeing

'Your methods WORK! My son is not yet 14 months old, and is generally pretty happy, but it's amazing how quickly the crying stops when I tell him I know what it is he's trying to say (which is usually pretty obvious – I want that toy; I don't want to be in bed), instead of trying to placate him with "It's OK" or "There, there". Amazing. You've got a legion of groupies now, with my extended family who look after him while I'm working. Thank you!'

Elisa
Mother of one

About the author

Dr Justin Coulson is a parenting, relationships and happiness expert. He is a Research Fellow at the Illawarra Institute for Mental Health in the School of Psychology at the University of Wollongong, and also acts as an Honorary Research Fellow at the Australian Institute of Business Wellbeing. Justin completed his Bachelor of Psychological Science with first-class honours at the University of Queensland, and received his PhD, researching parenting and happiness, from the University of Wollongong. Justin lectures in the psychology of wellbeing at UOW, and has had his research published in academic journals and peer reviewed books.

Justin appears regularly as a parenting expert in the media, including on The TODAY show, on ABC local radio, Radio National and in various newspapers, magazines and blogs. For over ten years, Justin has been providing happiness, relationship and parenting training to parents, teachers and the corporate sector. Clients have included various church groups, preschools, schools and major corporates.

Justin and his wife Kylie are the parents of five daughters. They live near Wollongong, New South Wales.

Acknowledgements

I have been fortunate in the course of my parenting journey to find superb information from two people who consistently question the standard parenting paradigms we operate under, and suggest scientifically sound alternatives: Professor H. Wallace Goddard and Alfie Kohn. I owe a great debt to their writing and influence. I particularly acknowledge Wally Goddard's kindness and generosity in sharing his wisdom with me personally, and becoming a cherished friend. Both Wally and Alfie's influences can be found in this book.

I appreciate Terri Cornish's interest in my work, and her willingness when we first met to talk with me for what must have been hours while she was manning an ACER Press stand at a parenting conference. I owe this book, in many ways, to Terri, who liked what I had to say and pitched the book to Debbie Lee at ACER.

To Debbie and Annemarie, I thank you for saying 'yes' to a guy with an idea and a passion for parenting and for reading initial drafts of the manuscript. To Elisa, for your way with words and editorial experience, you made shredding my work and leaving cherished stories and ideas on the editing room floor much more enjoyable than it sounds. Thank you for your attention to detail. I appreciate the many parents whose stories are told in this book. Their challenges, mistakes and successes are revealed in detail for all of us to learn from. I am grateful to them for allowing me to use their lives as our lesson.

To Mum and Dad, thank you for believing in me and offering your wisdom. More importantly, thank you for your example, and your unconditional love and support. And to my brother, Tim, for sharing your talent in allowing your photography to cover this book, thanks.

All of my best advice about parenting has gone into this book, which means that all of the experiences I have with my children get measured against what I have written – perhaps not by other people, but certainly by me. So I thank each of my five children. Chanel, Abbie, Ella, Annie and Lilli, you girls are my world and I pray that I will live up to the high standards a father should reach in raising such precious souls.

To my wife, Kylie, I express my deepest appreciation. Kylie has shown unwavering faith in me throughout our lives together. I am indebted to her for her enduring love, unwavering trust and unending support and belief.

Contents

Preface

It is said that we are drawn towards studying the things that we most need to practise in our own lives. In 2002, I realised that I needed to learn some things about parenting. My wife, Kylie, and I had a two-year-old daughter, and we were expecting our second child in just a few months. It was a Saturday afternoon, and Kylie had gone to the shops, leaving me at home with our two-year-old, Chanel. For reasons now forgotten, Chanel was upset and making a terrible fuss. She was screaming and kicking, throwing a classic two-year-old tantrum. I tried to calm Chanel down, to distract her, to play with her, all to no avail. The crying got worse. I had a terrible headache, having been up late the night before, and awake early and at work that morning.

After a short period of trying 'everything' (which is what parents always say they've done before they snap), I snapped. Chanel was punished. I smacked her. I locked her in her room. I listened to her scream. I yelled at her. I did all the things that frustrated parents do when they don't know what else to do. And I felt awful for it. I felt as though I had betrayed this tiny little girl who just wanted her Dad to 'get' that she needed him.

Chanel finally fell asleep in her room, but the nagging pain inside me refused to settle. It lingered. Over a decade later, it still distresses me.

Frustrated with myself, I stepped into the backyard to try and work things out in my mind. I had been a willing partner in starting my family, but my inability to cope with my daughter made me feel that I wasn't prepared to be a parent. I had been excited about it, but now that reality was biting, I found that I was ill-equipped. I had no ready answers. I was learning that I had little patience, and a drastic lack of skills. (Of course, before we'd had Chanel I thought I knew exactly how children should be raised – I even shared my opinions with a few parents whose children were challenging them … Oops).

While I battled my conscience in the backyard, a new battle commenced in a house a few doors down. The whole neighbourhood could hear it. It made my earlier conflict with Chanel sound like a polite discussion. A father had completely lost it with his young child. The screaming child and the hollering father left my stomach churning and my heart hollow. While the scene dwarfed my own poor parenting exhibition, it felt like my experience was being replayed, amplified, for all to hear. I was embarrassed, ashamed and all too aware of how my actions had hurt my little girl.

That was a turning point in my life. I began researching parenting. Within twelve months I had quit my radio career and enrolled in a psychology degree. I then completed a PhD in parenting, meaning in life and happiness. And now, I teach parenting.

In the past twenty to thirty years, parenting has become a topic of significant focus in our society. We have discovered just how important it is that we get it 'right' – the way we raise our babies into adults affects our children, their children and society more generally. This knowledge has increased the pressure on parents. Often we place that pressure upon ourselves. Then, when we make mistakes, we judge ourselves harshly. But while there are many things we *might* do to raise happy children, there are really just a handful of things we *need* to do. If we develop these skills and attributes as best we can, our families will flourish.

Chapter One outlines our children's need for us to simply 'be there'. Our emotional availability is one of the greatest contributions we can make to any relationship.

Chapter Two describes communication in families, and the incredible need our children have to be understood.

Chapter Three describes discipline with a difference. Many parents believe that disciplining children is about punishing them. Discipline solutions that have far greater impact over the long term are provided in this chapter, but they really only work effectively if the principles outlined in the first two parts of the book are followed.

Finally, Chapter Four has been written as a reminder of what really matters in parenting, and brings all of the other parts together to show how they build happy families.

This book is for every parent, regardless of the age of your children. All of your relationships can be improved using the ideas in this book, including your connections with your young children, your adult children, your spouse, your siblings, your parents and even your co-workers. The stories that are told are all true, and come from the many workshops, counselling sessions and discussions I have had with thousands of parents over the years. Only the names of the people have been changed.

When I started on this path, good parenting was what I most needed to learn. In many ways it is still what I most need to learn. I still make mistakes. My children continue to push my buttons and, from time to time, I still crack. Some days are better than others for all of us, whether we're experts or novices; whether we're single parents, or in a relationship with another adult who can offer support. The amazing thing I've discovered about parenting is that it is really a self-development course for *adults*. Our children teach us things about ourselves we might never otherwise learn. Perhaps, more than anything, they can teach us to become truly kind, compassionate people – if we make it a priority. The men and women who shape history are shaped by you and me – mums and dads. We all want a happy family. This book will show you how to have one.

How to read this book

Parents are busy. It can be difficult to find the time to settle into a comfortable chair and read. Of course, if your child sees you pick up a book and sit down somewhere cosy, you are sure to have their attention. Looking comfortable and relaxed is a guaranteed way to have your children trying to climb on you, play with you or talk to you.

Because parents have so much to do, this book is short, simple and to the point. While it could have been twice as long, I wanted to give you the best information in concise snippets so you can read a handful of pages before bed, get some easy ideas and inspiration and close the book before any children notice that you've disappeared to read.

You will get the most out of the book by reading it from cover to cover, but there might be certain sections that really interest you, and skipping straight to those points may provide you with some answers and solutions that are helpful. Then, in time, you can work back through the remainder of the book.

There are several places in each chapter where you will be invited to take some time to think through 'points to ponder'. I recognise that not everyone likes to interrupt their reading to think through ideas, and I also know that children can make any kind of introspection a challenge. While I recommend that you do take the time to ponder the suggestions given, if you feel that it is not your 'thing' or if circumstances don't permit, then read the book in the way that makes you feel most comfortable.

You will also see boxes that help you with 'putting it into practice'. The point of reading a book about parenting is to work out useful ways to do things better. These boxes will give you a range of ideas to practise, and to make your family happier.

If finding time to sit down with a book proves too difficult, you can listen to the audio version, available on CD or in MP3 format from http://shop.acer.edu.au.

Enjoy the book. And feel free to contact me if you have any feedback, via my email, justin@happyfamilies.com.au. I'd love to hear from you.

Points to ponder

Take a few minutes to respond to these questions. You may want to write down your ideas, talk with someone or just pause and think.

- Think of a specific time when have you been at your absolute best as a parent. How did you feel? What were you thinking? What were you doing?
- Consider all the things that made it possible for you to be like that. How can you get there again?

Mummy, Daddy, I need you!

1

'In family life, be completely present.'
Lao Tzu[1]

We all have those nights …

We're running late, dinner is burning, the phone is ringing and at least one child is dramatically upset. As we push through the frantic chaos, we become aware of our toddler, vying for some attention amid the stress.

'I know you want me, I'll be right there', we say as we race past our little one for the third time.

'Just let me take care of this and I'll be with you.'

'I hear you … I'm coming in just a minute.'

Finally, in a burst of exasperation these words cut through the noise and endless to-do list: 'Mummy (or Daddy) … I *need* you!'

In the busyness of family life, we often get so absorbed by the *things* around us that we overlook the deeply dependent little human beings that need our attention. As parents, we are valuable, indispensable, needed. Sometimes it would be nice to not be so needed. Life would be so much simpler if we could clock off for the day at 8 pm, like an employee. But parenting doesn't work like that. It is an on-call, 24-hour-a-day, non-stop role. The ongoing, always-at-the-ready, nature of being a parent makes it extremely challenging to always be emotionally available for our children. But that is precisely what they need – a parent who is *emotionally available*. This is the single most important thing we can do to create a happy, peaceful home and a secure child.

How to build a real relationship with your child

The story below is one of the most remarkable stories I have experienced in working with parents and I am often asked whether it is true. It is, and it underscores just how critical this principle of emotional availability is for every child.

I was teaching my Happy Families workshop to a group of parents in Brisbane. It was the second week of a four-week program. The previous week, we had discussed the idea of being emotionally available to our children, and every parent had committed to looking for ways that they could do this before the next session. In following this commitment up, I asked for people to share their recent experiences of being emotionally available and Jenny tentatively raised her hand.

Jenny was a mother of three children. She was embarrassed to say that she typically didn't make time for her seven-year-old daughter, Emily. It wasn't that Emily was neglected. It was just that she bothered Jenny – a lot. Jenny loved her daughter, but, she confessed, she didn't really *like* Emily very much. It had always been that way, almost as if she had never properly bonded with her eldest child.

Jenny was mowing the lawn on the Saturday morning following our Friday evening workshop when Emily approached. It was a bad time. Jenny didn't enjoy this kind of work and she didn't want be interrupted with 'daughter issues'.

'This is just typical of Emily!', thought Jenny. 'Why does she have to bother me right now?' Her daughter's presence was a consistently unwelcome intrusion. But then she remembered the commitment she had made in our workshop the previous evening: 'For the next week I will do whatever it takes to be emotionally available to my children, if and when they need me'.

Being emotionally available sounded so simple in the parenting session. It just meant stopping what she was doing and paying attention to her children. Somewhat reluctantly, Jenny switched off the mower, and together mother and daughter went to the front yard where they sat on a rock in the shade.

Emily was characteristically unhappy. Jenny told us of the effort she had to make to really be there. She looked directly into Emily's eyes. She silently reconfirmed her commitment. 'I will be emotionally available to my children when they need me.'

'What do you want to talk about, Emily?'

After a lengthy pause, perhaps in an attempt to ascertain her mum's degree of sincerity, this little seven-year-old finally whispered a need that had been unresolved for some time.

'Mummy, I just don't know why I'm here or where I fit in our family. Sometimes I feel like you don't really love me.'

Can you imagine how you might feel to hear your child share such lonely, deeply heartfelt feelings? Jenny broke down as she shared this experience. It was, in her words, 'really full on'.

Sitting with her daughter in the shade, Jenny shut out her other priorities and listened as Emily shared her feelings, fears and a desire to feel a part of her family. Jenny did not try to persuade her daughter that she was being silly. She did not try to fix the problem. Instead she simply stayed right there in the moment. She listened to Emily, felt what she was feeling, and held her close when she needed it.

Jenny explained that it had been a huge effort to stop what she was doing and take the time to be emotionally available. She had not wanted to. She had resisted. But because she was able to be fully present, a connection was created, a conversation was shared and a little girl felt, for the first time, just how important she really was to her mother. For Jenny, this was a watershed moment. She described how the experience led her to recognise deep feelings of love that she did not know she had for Emily.

Points to ponder

- Think of a time when someone was really 'there' for you. Describe (or imagine) everything you can about the situation.
  - How was the person showing you s/he was emotionally available?
  - What words encouraged you?
  - What body language made you feel safe and heard?
  - How did it make you feel about the thing that was troubling you?
  - How did it make you feel about the person who was available to you?
- Think of a time when you were able to respond in such a way for your children. Describe how it felt for you. And consider how it felt for your children.
  - How do you know your children sensed your availability?
  - What words did you use?

»

> – What body language made your children feel safe and heard?
> – How did it make your children feel about the thing that was troubling them?
> – How did your children respond to you?

PUTTING IT INTO PRACTICE

· Consciously make yourself emotionally available for your children more often. Look for opportunities to really be there for your children.

Resilience

Resilience is the capacity that we have to 'bounce back' from setbacks, challenges and difficulties in our lives. One of the most significant findings in childrearing research[2] is that children are far more resilient when they have at least one person in their lives who is 'there' for them. Almost without exception, children who grow up to be most resilient have one significant person in their lives who knows what it is to be emotionally available, and who takes the time to do so. Children who grow up this way develop what psychologists call a 'secure attachment'. This means that they feel emotionally and physically safe, and they view the world and relationships as positive and exciting places that are there to be explored.

As a contrast, almost without exception, children who grow up at the other end of the resilience spectrum never know what it is like to have someone who is 'there', who offers consistent, pervasive nurture and love. Children who grow up without this significant influence in their lives generally develop an 'insecure attachment', which means that they feel emotionally insecure. They view relationships with suspicion, as though they are transactions to be made. The world becomes a frightening place where people cannot be trusted. Such children rarely thrive.

Emmy Werner is a developmental psychologist who completed a study of high-risk children in a community on the Hawaiian island of Kauai that has become a psychology classic, and provides one of the most important lessons in helping us know what leads to flourishing adults. Dr Werner found a community that was populated by a heavy proportion of high-risk families. Within the community that she studied, poverty, unemployment, drug and alcohol addiction, teenage pregnancy and family breakdown were all too common. Werner followed the 698 children born in that community in 1955, gathering data from them and their parents. Her study continued for over forty years, collecting information through interviews and questionnaires in relation to the children's wellbeing and life outcomes.

A full two-thirds of the high-risk children struggled to cope with life as they grew. They were not resilient. They fell into the dominant destructive patterns so prevalent in their community. They did poorly at school. They experienced mood and anxiety disorders. They were involved with drugs or alcohol, often to the point of abuse. They became parents, often in their teenage years, and were generally ineffective in their parenting responsibilities.

But one third of the high-risk children were able to cope successfully with the challenges they experienced. Werner discovered that among those who developed successfully there were four factors that led to positive outcomes. First, the children who grew up well had a close personal relationship – a secure attachment – with a parent or another mature adult who was there for them. Second, they had positive experiences with school. Third, they were part of a religious community that helped them have a sense of coherence about their lives. And fourth, they had at least one close friend that could give them emotional support. The single most critical protective factor for successful coping and development was a positive relationship between the child and another adult. This research has been replicated on smaller scales with data from Australia[3], Denmark[4], Sweden[5], Germany[6], New Zealand[7] and the USA[8]. The findings remain consistent. Children need that one person to be available to them. That person, ideally, should be YOU.

The little things

I was once asked by a mother, 'What do you think the most important thing might be for a mum to do?'

'What do you think?', was my reply. She had been preparing for a mother's group discussion on being a mum, so she was ready with her

»

answers. Her ideas included helping the children develop, teaching them, caring for them, working to maintain various aspects of the home, reading to her children, being a good role model, providing discipline and setting limits and many other worthy suggestions. But none pinpointed my ready response.

I suggested that more than anything, children need parents who will *always* be there for them, and who will love them no matter what. I told this mum that the best way we can show our love is to be available to our children. As if to provide supporting evidence, the next day this mum had the following interaction with her six-year-old daughter:

Mother: 'What do you like doing most with mum?'
Sienna: 'I don't really care what I do with you. I just like to spend time with you.'
Mother: 'Doing what, though?'
Sienna: 'Doesn't matter. I just like to be with you.'

Kids don't need fancy treats, holidays and piles of toys. They respond poorly when they are indulged. Instead, they need parents to be there for them, and to love them like crazy; to be emotionally available. That is the foundation of building a relationship with your child. It really is that simple. Trevor's story illustrates this point.

After saving enough money, Trevor sat down with his children and told them he was taking them on a holiday to America. They would go to Disneyland, and a whole bunch of other places that the children promptly forgot. Who can remember anything when you are being told you are going to Disneyland?

The two-week holiday was frenetic. The children and their dad did everything they had planned to do. They arrived home in Australia exhausted. The day before school resumed, Trevor decided to use his last day off work with his children and travelled around his city on one of the free buses that operated. The bus took a thirty-minute loop around the city, through the CBD, past the beaches, out to the University and back into the city. Given that his budget was obliterated after his overseas holiday, a free bus ride with the kids seemed a perfectly-priced entertainment option.

The following day, as Trevor took his children to the school gate, the family was stopped by a teacher. Knowing how excited the children had been about their overseas holiday, she asked the children how their trip had been. The children excitedly responded that it had been wonderful.

'What was the best part of the holidays?', the teacher asked.
'My favourite thing was going on the bus with my Dad yesterday. We just sat on the bus and watched everything and talked.'
Trevor's jaw dropped!

In his own words, the day before school had started, Trevor had done nothing. He had given his children a free ride on a bus, and his undivided attention for a little over thirty minutes. But the impact it had on his daughter was dramatic. That single experience had been a better, bigger highlight than a trip to Disneyland just a week earlier.

It may be true that the bus ride was simply the first thing his daughter thought of. After all, it had only happened yesterday. Disneyland did come up in the conversation and was also appreciated, but on reflection, Trevor recognised that the entire time they spent in the United States, he was rushing and stressed. He was worried about keeping his children safe and close; worried about food, sleep, accommodation and money. Directions and being lost plagued his experience and increased his stress levels. He spent a lot of time with his children, but he wasn't present. There was too much pressure.

Comparatively, the bus ride was simple, quiet and he was really *there*.

PUTTING IT INTO PRACTICE

· Look for opportunities to spend time (not money) on your children. The simpler, the better. Sitting in the backyard, pushing them on a swing or walking around the neighbourhood are great examples of just being there with them.

Be where your feet are

Mindful parenting

The idea of being mindful has received a lot of attention from psychologists in recent years. It seems that mindfulness has a strong relationship with our wellbeing, and that of our children. Mindfulness is being aware of what is happening right now and remaining focused on that. It's being *present* in the present. Mindfulness requires us to 'be where our feet are'.

Parents who are emotionally available make a conscious decision to be mindful. They are aware of their children's needs and respond attentively. When a child comes to them with a request, a mindful parent stops ... and listens. A mindful parent does not necessarily indulge the child, give in or be at the child's beck and call. Instead, mindful parents attempt to comprehend their children's emotional state, and respond in a deliberate and careful manner.

Children who experience mindful parenting agree to statements like these:

My parents support me.
My parents console me when I am upset.
My parents show they care about me.
My parents show a genuine interest in me.
My parents remember things that are important to me.
My parents are available to talk at any time.
My parents ask questions in a caring manner.
My parents spend extra time with me just because they want to.
My parents are willing to talk about my troubles.
My parents talk with me about my interests.
My parents value my input.
My parents make me feel wanted.

Point to ponder

Take a moment and pretend that you are your child. Would you agree with the above statements about you? Would your children agree with those statements?

Decades of research indicate that children who have parents who take the time to be there for them experience the following:

Greater self-confidence and self-esteem	If a child has parents who are available to him, he will be more likely to believe that he is a person who is worthy and valuable. People who feel that they are valued are able to approach the world confidently.[9]

Resilience	When a child encounters challenges and setbacks she will typically return to her parents for comfort and support. Knowing that she can be validated and supported helps her 'bounce back' from setbacks and try again. Emotionally available parents have resilient children.[10]
Learning outcomes	Children who have parents who take the time to be emotionally available show a greater interest in learning than children whose parents aren't there for them. This, in turn, leads to better academic performance.[11]
Social skills	Children with emotionally available parents have better peer relations. This is perhaps because when parents are emotionally available, they model positive social skills and children follow these examples in their own relationships. These children are also more accepted by their peers and other adults, including their teachers.[12]
Emotional regulation	When a child is comforted, or has a parent who is attentive, she learns to regulate powerful emotions more effectively because her parents guide her through them. This means that as she gets older, she is familiar enough with the experience of powerful emotions to deal with them effectively on her own.[13]

It's not a bad list, is it? In short, kids whose parents are mindful of their emotional needs and take the time to engage with them when needed are more confident, happier, better adjusted, do better at school and cope with life's challenges more effectively.

Mindless parenting

The alternative to being emotionally available is to be emotionally disengaged. When we are emotionally disengaged, we ignore our children and refuse to involve ourselves in their lives. Our responses to our children's needs are automatic, with little or no awareness of what is occurring within our child. Author Alfie Kohn calls this kind of parenting operating on 'autoparent'.[14] This happens at those times when we brush our children off, giving them a cursory 'uh-huh' while we listen to our own thoughts and respond to our own needs.

All of us are guilty of operating on autoparent at times and, while not ideal, disengagement is completely normal. No parent can be endlessly involved in everything their children are doing, thinking, saying and feeling. In fact, for our households to function effectively it is necessary, and healthy, to allow our children space. Being emotionally available does not mean hovering over our children, or 'helicopter parenting'. What matters most is our availability when we are needed. The best parents find a way to be emotionally available and present for their child *when the need does arise*. All other priorities can be put off. The child becomes the focus, and the parent becomes mindful: present and aware.

When parents are emotionally absent from their children on a consistent basis, this mindlessness leads to outcomes that are diametrically opposed to the positive ones described earlier. Children who come from families where parents are pervasively emotionally disengaged are likely to answer 'no' to many of the questions in the list on p. 8. These children are at significant risk of experiencing various behavioural and psychological problems.

Some issues surface at a relatively young age. These can include challenging behaviours, talking back, oppositional behaviour or just being moody, irritable and easily upset. However, the fruits of pervasive disengagement and parents' emotional unavailability take several years to develop.[15] By early or mid-adolescence, these problems can include:

Internalising issues	Psychologists use the phrase 'internalising' to describe the way that someone takes 'in' what is going on in their world. When children are consistently emotionally neglected, they internalise this rejection or dismissiveness from their parents. Ultimately it can lead to internal issues such as depression, anxiety or other mood disorders, or problems such as anorexia.
Violence and delinquent activity	Children who feel like their emotional needs are unmet find a variety of ways to express their pain. Anger, aggression and destruction are an easy way for these children to demonstrate their difficulties. Of course, such behaviour typically gets them attention – but not the attention they need.

Drug use and abuse	When children feel disengaged, they will turn to alternative activities to alleviate the feeling of being unimportant in someone's life. Drugs fill that void for many of these children.
Early promiscuity and sexual activity	To compensate for a perceived lack of love in their lives, relationships are formed that go too deep, too soon. Research has consistently demonstrated that boys and girls become physically involved at a younger age when their parents are emotionally disengaged. This is particularly true for girls who do not feel connected with their fathers.

Emotional availability, and specifically being mindful of our children's needs, makes a positive difference in the lives of all children, including those who are challenging and disruptive. It also has a significant positive influence on autistic children, reducing aggression, self harm and non-compliance.[16] Children with disabilities also been shown to become more social and less aggressive when their parents make the time to be mindful, and tend to their emotional needs as well.[17] In all cases, families function better when parents take the time and make the effort to be aware and available to their children.

Emotional bandwidth

A good friend of mine is a computer expert. Many years ago, he was explaining to me why my tired old computer would not work well when I tried to use the internet (which was still only just catching on in some places – my household included). It seemed that I had a bandwidth issue. Bandwidth, loosely defined, is the maximum amount of data that can be transferred from a server (or storage unit) to a computer in one second. I was using an old 56k modem, which, as the name suggests, allowed me to receive a maximum of 56 kilobits per second. I was not sure exactly how big a kilobit was, but he assured me it wasn't very much. ADSL internet had just become available and it allowed a bandwidth of up to 1.5 megabits per second. He confirmed that this was substantially greater than what I was currently able to access, and suggested that increasing my bandwidth connection would bring an end to my frustration.

As parents, we deal with problems of *emotional* bandwidth when it comes to raising our children. There are only so many things we can deal with at any one time. Once our bandwidth becomes clogged with the pressures of our busy lives, we struggle to be available to our children. We must recognise that we all have different capacities. Some of us may have a lower emotional bandwidth; one thing to focus on is enough. Work, running the house and looking after the children may be too much, without adding in a dog, monitoring piano practice, netball training, play dates for the children and a telephone that keeps on ringing. Conversely, some of us may have bandwidth capacity that is simply amazing, with the ability to do all of those things, as well as the energy for ninety minutes of exercise a day, taking meals to elderly neighbours, making thank you cards for the children's teachers, baking special lunch treats for the children's lunchboxes each day of the week and so on. And while emotional bandwidth varies from person to person, it also varies at different times throughout the day. Most of us experience 'peak' times around six o'clock each evening when it is dinner and bath time. Everyone is tired from a big day. Children are emotional. Our bandwidth is stretched in all directions.

I was attempting to do a little more around the house to help my wife, Kylie, before the impending birth of our fourth child. Without telling her, I decided to look after the clothes washing. I was off to a good start, with whites all in one pile and coloured items in another. Extra points to me because I took all of the delicate and wool items out of the general washing pile too.

Our washing machine was large. We needed it. Our family was getting bigger. At the time, the area where we lived was experiencing a prolonged drought. Being mindful of the environment, I was determined that the machine would not run unless it was full. I loaded it up, poured in the powder, pushed the buttons and congratulated myself on my domestic prowess.

An hour or so later the machine stopped. I emptied the clothes into the basket and went outside to hang them up. I was surprised, and more than a little disappointed, to find that the washing was not properly cleaned. I had done everything the right way, but something had gone wrong.

I began to browse the whitegoods catalogues. It was time for a new machine! Kylie noticed my interest in the electrical appliance junk mail, and after a brief discussion she had the problem diagnosed. It appeared that I had put too much clothing into the machine. In my efforts to conserve water and be efficient, I was now going to have to wash all of the clothes again, this time in two loads instead of one.

The lesson in this is simple: for a happy family, don't try to stuff too much in. You'll get better results for yourself and your family if you work within your capacity, physically and psychologically. The more we let ourselves become overwhelmed with life and all that it demands of us, the less emotionally available we are able to be for our children.

> ## Points to ponder
> - What things stop you being emotionally available for your children?
> - What specific things can you do – starting immediately – to overcome distracters that lead to emotional unavailability?

PUTTING IT INTO PRACTICE
- Decide on one or two changes you can make and commit to them now.
- If you keep a diary or journal, you will find it exciting to note the specific changes you experience as a result of being more available.

In my parenting workshops, I ask parents to make a list of the things that are in their lives that stop them being emotionally available to their children. Here is a sample of the answers that I receive:
- selfishness
- modelling (repeating what our parents did to us)
- lack of time
- running late
- other children making demands or 'needing' us
- television
- telephone
- internet
- tasks to complete
- having a bad day
- feeling frustrated and angry
- relationship conflict
- children behaving in a challenging way
- work stress
- financial stress

- not understanding our children
- not being able to consider our children's unique temperament.

It takes commitment and hard work to be an emotionally available parent. To do so we must proactively decide what we will eliminate to free up emotional bandwidth. One of the best ways to do this is to reduce our distractions. Here are a few ideas for how to clear unnecessary distractions from our parenting commitments:

- utilise support networks
- accept help
- create a schedule and stick to it, but be flexible
- work together, as partners and as a family
- remember your experiences as a child
- get some 'me' time
- if you are in a relationship, date your spouse. One of the most important things we can do for our children and our families is to keep our relationships strong.

> **Points to ponder**
>
> Review the ideas above, one by one. Do it slowly and ask yourself these questions:
>
> - Can I do this? If so, how?
> - Would it work for me?
> - When will I do it?
> - How can I know it has worked?

Here are some more quick tips for how to be more available:

- turn off the television
- eat at least one meal together each day
- have one night each week set in concrete as family time – no phone, internet or television
- stop, and just listen

- don't listen to the talkback radio when driving with the kids. Either keep the radio off, or listen to something you can all agree on, enjoy and even sing along to
- get enough sleep
- look after your body
- focus on your children when you're with them
- dance and play and run and have fun
- give yourself a daily 'holiday'. Prioritise twenty to thirty minutes each day that is 'me time'. This builds your emotional stockpiles, unclutters your bandwidth and gives you something to look forward to
- be willing to schedule adult tasks when children are in bed
- make an effort to understand what your children really want or need, rather than jumping to early conclusions about what you think they want or need.

The most important things aren't things

It can be challenging to make ourselves available for our children, to reduce the many things that are clogging up our bandwidth and to be where our feet are. A group of parents was agonising over how hard this can be during one of my workshops. Night-time schedules were a particular stress for some of these parents. Their idea of a perfect night required structure. Dinner was to be eaten at 6 pm, then the table was to be cleared and the dishes washed, dried and put away. This sounded reasonable to most of the parents in the room.

But one couple who were concerned about the issue said that while they cleaned up the kitchen, their young children would tear around the house, make a bigger mess and be generally disruptive. They weren't 'bad' kids. They were tired, unsupervised and were doing whatever they could to amuse themselves while they waited for their parents to clean up. Their parents had tried involving them in the tidy-up process, but all attempts had proven futile. The kids were too young and too tired.

As the parents discussed this dilemma, I quipped, 'Well, save the important stuff – like the dishes – until after the kids are in bed'.

When we minimise distractions and become emotionally available, we make the space for enriching moments that connect us with our children. When these parents recognised that a kitchen sink full of dishes could wait half an hour, they created space in their lives for the *genuinely* important things. They were able to spend both quality and quantity time with their children after their evening meal, bathing, brushing teeth, singing songs and reading stories. The dishes still got done. The parents had simply restructured their evening, deciding that the really important things were not the 'things' at all. The important things were their children.

> Meg Whitman is a successful businesswoman who has headed companies such as eBay and Hewlett Packard. Her net worth is more than one billion dollars. In an interview, Meg was asked what her biggest regret was. After some thought, she replied, 'Probably not spending as much time with the kids ... I did miss certain parts of their development. I wasn't there to see some of the really fun things that they did. So I suppose the biggest regret is ... it would be really great to have spent more time with them, particularly when they were little ... And you can't get that back'.
>
> Meg went on to say that, in terms of juggling parenthood, careers, money and everything else, you can't have it 'all'. She said, 'I think you can have a wonderful life, but you have to decide what trade-offs you're willing to make'.[18]

A favourite quote of mine goes like this: 'Kids spell love, T-I-M-E'. You may have noticed that whenever you invite your children into your world, to help with cooking, to wrestle on the floor or to simply take a walk, the children accept your gift with relish. They love being with their parents.

But if 'time' means 'love' to a child, what does 'hurry' mean? Hurry is the opposite of being emotionally available. Hurry tells a child, 'My needs are more important than yours'. It says, 'You are slowing me down', 'You're not pulling your weight', 'You are a burden'. Often our demands that our children hurry are the result of poor planning, impatience or intolerance. We can hurry them up, or we can embrace their enthusiasm for exploration, learning and new experiences. We can rush by with all of the other important things going on in our lives, or we can be emotionally available.

PUTTING IT INTO PRACTICE

· Set two goals that you will achieve this week in order to be more available to your children. Be as specific as possible. Describe the exact things you will do to make the changes.
· How will you know that you have succeeded?

A mum who attended one of my workshops recounted the following story:

> After learning about being emotionally available with my children, I decided that I would turn off the television at meal times and that we would talk. One night I asked my children what had been good about their day. As they talked I felt great to be having these conversations with them. When it was my eldest daughter's turn to tell me about what the best part of the day was, she looked at me and quietly said, 'Right now, mum'.

Notes

1 L Tzu, *Tao Te Ching*, verse 8, trans. S Mitchell, Frances Lincoln Limited, London, 1999.
2 EE Werner, 'What can we learn about resilience from large-scale longitudinal studies?', in S Goldstein & RB Brooks (eds), *Handbook of resilience in children*, Springer, New York, 2006, pp. 91–106.
3 P Brennan, R Le Broque & C Hammen, 'Resilience in children of depressed mothers: a focus on psychological, behavioural and social outcomes at age 15 years', paper presented at the meeting of the Society for Life History Research in Psychopathology, New York, September 2002.
4 J Parnas, TD Cannon, B Jacobsen, H Schulsinger, F Schulsinger & SA Mednick, 'Lifetime DSM-III-R diagnostic outcomes in the offspring of schizophrenic mothers: results from the Copenhagen high-risk study', *Archives of General Psychiatry*, vol. 50, no. 9, 1993, pp. 707–14.
5 M Cederblad, 'The children of the Lundby study as adults: a salutogenic perspective', *European Child & Adolescent Psychiatry*, vol. 5, supp. 1, 1996, pp. 38–43.
6 F Losel & T Bliesener, 'Resilience in adolescence: a study on the generalizability of protective factors', in K Hurrelmann and F Losel (eds), *Health hazards in adolescence*, Walter De Gruyter, Oxford, 1990, pp. 299–320.
7 A Caspi, K Sugden, TE Moffitt, A Taylor, IW Craig, H Harrington, J McClay, J Mill, J Martin, A Braithwaite & R Poulton, 'Influence of life stress on depression: moderation by a polymorphism in the 5-HTT gene', *Science*, vol. 301, no. 5631, pp. 386–89.
8 AS Masten & JL Powell, 'A resilience framework for research, policy, and practice', in SS Luthar (ed), *Resilience and vulnerability: adaptation in the context of childhood adversities*, Cambridge University Press, New York, 2003, pp. 1–25.
TM Yates, B Egeland & LA Sroufe, 'Rethinking resilience: a developmental process perspective' in SS Luthar (ed), *Resilience and vulnerability: adaptation in the context of childhood adversities*, Cambridge University Press, New York, 2003, pp. 243–66.
9 JM Gottman, *Raising an emotionally intelligent child*, Simon & Schuster, New York, 1998.
10 EE Werner & RE Smith, *Journeys from childhood to midlife: risk, resilience and recovery*, Cornell University Press, Ithaca, 2001.

11 WA Goldberg, E Greenberger & SK Nagel, 'Employment and achievement: mothers' work involvement in relation to children's achievement behaviors and mothers' parenting behaviours', *Child Development*, vol. 67, no. 4, 1996, pp. 1512–27.
    JF Sorce & RN Emde, 'Mother's presence is not enough: effect of emotional availability on infant exploration', *Developmental Psychology*, vol. 17, no. 6, 1981, pp. 737–45.

12 DB Bugental & JE Grusec, 'Socialization processes', in N Eisenberg, W Damon & RM Lerner (eds), *Handbook of child psychology: Vol. 3, Social, emotional and personality development*, 6th edn, John Wiley & Sons, Hoboken, New Jersey, 2006, pp. 366–428.
    EE Maccoby, 'The role of parents in the socialization of children: an historical overview', *Developmental Psychology*, vol. 28, no. 6, 1992, pp. 1006–17.

13 BL Volling, NL McElwain, PC Notaro & C Herrera, 'Parents' emotional availability and infant emotional competence: predictors of parent-infant attachment and emerging self-regulation', *Journal of Family Psychology*, vol. 16, no. 4, 2002, pp. 447–65.

14 A Kohn, *Unconditional Parenting: moving from rewards and punishments to love and reason*, Atria Books, New York, 2005.

15 BA van der Kolk, JC Perry & JL Herman, 'Childhood origins of self-destructive behaviour', *American Journal of Psychiatry*, vol. 148, no. 12, 1991, pp. 1665–71.

16 AH Rutgers, MJ Bakermans-Kranenburg, MH van Ijzendoorn, & IA van Berckelaer-Onnes, 'Autism and attachment: a meta-analytic review', *Journal of Child Psychology and Psychiatry*, vol. 45, no. 6, 2004, pp. 1123–34.
    L Seskin, E Feliciano, G Tippy, R Yedloutschnig, KM Sossin & A Yasik, 'Attachment and autism: parental attachment representations and relational behaviors in the parent–child dyad', *Journal of Abnormal Child Psychology*, vol. 38, no. 7, 2010, pp. 949–60.

17 R Tessier, GM Tarabulsy, S Larin, J Laganière, M-F Gagnon & J Trahan, 'A home-based description of attachment in physically disabled infants', *Social Development*, vol. 11, no. 2, 2002, pp. 147–65.

18 JC Johnson, *I am a mother*, Deseret Book, Salt Lake City, Utah, 2010.

I Can't Understand My Kids: Why Won't They Listen to Me?

2

'One of the most obvious facts about grownups, to a child, is that they have forgotten what it is like to be a child.'
Randall Jarrell[1]

Parenting is about doing a lot of really simple things at difficult times. The first principle we have discussed – taking the time to be emotionally available – is a good example of this. It's a simple idea to talk about. It feels right and it's easy to understand. But to actually do this 'simple' thing can be really challenging. The second key principle is one that connects families: children need *to be understood*. In theory, taking the time to listen to and understand someone is another straightforward idea that makes intuitive sense. Of course we need to understand our kids. It sounds easy enough, but in practice, it can be difficult to implement. Here's an example:

> One evening, a family watched a movie together that contained some mildly scary themes, including a ghost. One of the children in the family was a ten-year-old girl. Watching the movie seemed like fun at the time, but when the lights went out at the end of the evening, the young girl was scared.
>
> As her parents put her into bed, Isabela resisted. She became clingy. She wanted cuddles, a story, a song, a drink and so on. Her parents found her behaviour tedious, but they remained attentive. Eventually, however,
>
> »

it moved beyond annoying. Isabela's parents were tired. She was stringing her bedtime out, and ruining what had been a pleasant evening. Their plans for the rest of the night did not include dealing with a scared ten-year-old girl refusing to sleep. Besides, they'd had a special family night.

'If this is how you are going to react to watching a silly movie', they warned, 'We just won't do these nights anymore'.

At this point, Isabela's parents could have shown that they understood that she was scared, and dealt with her fears compassionately. But their agenda got in the way. At a superficial level, they verbalised, 'Yes, Isabela, we know you're scared', but *recognising* an emotion and *understanding* it are two different things.

As the girl's fear and crying increased, the minutes turned into quarter-hours. Over an hour later, Isabela's parents had gone from annoyed, to exasperated, and now her dad was angry. Each parent had used all of the logic they could think of to help their daughter realise that there were no ghosts in their house. They had reasoned, bribed, threatened, yelled and demanded that she recognise how silly she was being, and calm down and go to sleep. Like most parents, they believed that they had done 'everything'.

At around ten o'clock, Isabela's father had finally had enough. It was two hours past her bedtime, and it was past his bedtime too. He pulled his daughter from her bed, grabbed her by the hand, and partly walked her, partly dragged her, around the outside perimeter of the house in the pitch dark of the late night. All the while she cried, screaming that the ghosts would 'get her'. He argued back, 'Where are the ghosts? There are NO ghosts!' Petrified, she was hauled back into her bedroom and told to go to sleep.

You can probably guess that Isabela didn't disturb her parents any more that evening. Instead, she spent the time until she fell asleep sobbing into her pillow. But was the problem settled in her mind? Did she feel any safer because her dad had proved that there were no ghosts around the house? Probably not – on both counts.

As I consider this story, I can't help but wonder whether that experience left Isabela feeling less scared of the ghosts and more scared of her father. In some small way, a dent was made in her relationship with her dad.

Trust was reduced. Emotional pain was inflicted rather than healed. If this experience was a one-off, then it probably would not have a significant impact on Isabela's feelings of safety and security. But if it became the standard way that her father dealt with her emotional pain, then their relationship would be strained, and her wellbeing would suffer.

The following story involving my nine-year-old daughter Abbie provides a useful contrast.

One afternoon, I was explaining to my eldest daughter, Chanel, why I was reluctant to allow her, at the age of twelve, to walk the three kilometres from our home to a major shopping centre nearby so that she could hang out. Chanel believed that she was old enough to enjoy the privilege, and that she would be safe. Chanel is a persistent negotiator, and after around twenty minutes of going back and forth I described to her the story of Daniel Morcombe.

Daniel was a thirteen-year-old boy when he was abducted. His remains were found in a forest near his home eight years after his disappearance, following one of the biggest missing persons cases in Australian history. I gently discussed this with Chanel, explaining that while the chances were extremely low that something like that might happen to her, it was a risk I was not prepared to take. Another couple of years would be needed before I would allow her to do what she was asking. We revisited the rules our family has about walking around the neighbourhood, we talked about other ways that Chanel might meet her goals of spending time with friends and going to the shops, and we agreed, together, that while she would probably be safe if she were to walk to the shops, it was better to stick with our rules for now.

That evening, as I said goodnight to the children, Chanel's younger sister, Abbie, was sniffling softly in her bed. She cuddled me longer than normal and told me she was upset. When I asked her why, she told me that she was scared something would happen to her in the same way that something had happened to Daniel Morcombe.

It would have been easy to reassure her things would be fine and leave the room. Similarly, it would have been easy to dismiss her statement by telling her not to be silly, reminding her of the rules we have to keep her safe, and then reassuring her that everything would be OK. Both responses could be considered warm and could show I was emotionally available – to a point. But both would also be dismissive, and Abbie probably would have remained insecure.

»

Instead, I knelt down beside Abbie and listened to her concerns. I spent time making sure she knew that I understood how she was feeling. We talked about how it feels to be worried, and why it feels like that. Within a few moments, Abbie was calm. Once her emotions were settled, we were able to have a useful discussion. I apologised for telling a story that upset her. And then, when the 'emotional first aid' (see p. 31) that comes through understanding her had done its job, we talked about her future. We talked about how confident we could both be that she would be fine, because she had her friends to be with, and a family to watch over her. We talked about her finishing primary school and going to high school, then perhaps university. We laughed about who she might marry, and the children she might have. Abbie was able to have a conversation that made her optimistic because she felt understood, and her emotions were settled.

Emotional flooding destroys understanding

Our children want to be understood. Combined with our emotional availability, it is their greatest need. When we take the time to recognise their feelings and show them that we understand them, they feel more in control of their feelings, and are easier to work with. Conversely, when we dismiss their feelings and do not show understanding, our children will often become emotional. Sometimes they'll externalise those emotions by acting out, crying or being challenging in some other way. Other times they'll toe the line, but internalise their emotions, bottling them up inside. Either way, as levels of emotion increase within our children, they eventually flood their little minds and bodies and stop them thinking rationally, or responding to us appropriately.

Here's an example of what happens when we are not understanding towards our children.

My family's routine in the morning requires our three school-aged girls to be up at 6.45 am and downstairs ready to get things happening by 7 am. That gives them a full fifteen minutes to dress themselves and make their beds. Considerable time, and they've proven on many occasions that it can be done with ease. But this particular morning was different. Even with regular reminders, pestering, nagging and restraint (on my part), it took three quarters of an hour, and me making their beds, before three pairs of feet slowly made their way down the steps into the lounge room. It was at about this point that my rational mind went missing.

> I explained, in a fairly noisy way, and with a much more aggressive tone than normal, that I was unhappy. And annoyed. And late. And that it was their fault! 'How hard can it be to get dressed in your school uniform?' I reminded the children that I had asked them at least half-a-dozen times to get moving, get dressed, get downstairs and get on with it.
>
> It seemed that my outburst, however shameful and embarrassing on my part, did the trick. They got moving. In fact, they were remarkably helpful for the next fifteen minutes.
>
> That's when the learning occurred for me. I called them together and apologised for being upset, and for speaking loudly (a euphemism for yelling), acknowledging that even dads who know better still make mistakes sometimes. Then I asked the question, 'What have you learned from what I said to you on the stairs?'
>
> The response was … well, actually there wasn't a response from any of the girls. So I asked again. And again, nothing. I could feel my blood pressure rising. Hadn't they learned anything? Had my angst been in vain? Had my lecture not provided them with the educational experience I had hoped for?
>
> Ella, aged six, sensed my growing frustration and perhaps her impending doom. She took a wild guess about what she thought I wanted her to have learned from our 'discussion'.
>
> 'I learned that I should be nice to my sisters?' Ella's response was as much a plea for approval as it was a hopeful stab in the dark.
>
> Wrong answer. I asked if they remembered anything at all that I had said.
>
> 'No.' Their three voices were almost inaudible. They had no idea what I had been angry about. I had a ten-year-old, a seven-year-old and a six-year-old in front of me. Each was developmentally capable of understanding basic instructions, and comprehending the things her parents said. But my anger had muted my children's ability to learn. All they could recall was that dad was angry. My words were meaningless because of their aroused nervous systems.

The angrier we get as parents, the less our children hear us say. Learning occurs best when we feel comfortable, safe and emotionally secure. When our children are scared, they only learn that the big person is scary. It's hard to learn anything, or understand much, when emotions are running high.

> If I could have my time over, it would have been far more effective for me to go to each of my daughters and describe how I sensed they felt.
>
> 'You seem tired this morning.'
>
> 'You would rather play than get ready for school. Playing with your toys is much more fun, isn't it?'
>
> 'You're annoyed that you can't find your clothes.'
>
> 'Your bed just won't get made this morning and it's frustrating you.'

Statements of understanding should always precede statements of teaching and instruction, or restating of limits, rules and directions. It is only after our children feel understood that they can listen, understand and make good decisions.

Points to ponder

Think of the last time someone upset you. Perhaps it was one of your children, a spouse or a colleague. While you were in the peak of your emotion were you able to listen to their apology, their explanation or their attempts to justify their behaviour? Were you creating counter-arguments, rationalising your indignation or letting the rage immerse you? Were you considering how the experience might make you a better person, or teach you?

When you become frustrated or angry with your children, what is your typical reaction? If you become aggressive, demonstrative or start yelling, what do you suspect your children get from what you do and say?

Emotions are contagious

High emotion causes flooding, and an inability to process thoughts effectively. High emotions are also contagious. Just like diseases, not everyone will 'catch' them, but there are few who are entirely immune. When our children have 'big' emotions, we as parents seem to catch the same emotion that our children have, or some variation of it. And when we express high emotionality, our children also experience it, and catch it instantly – often with unintended negative consequences. When this high level of emotion is experienced, it consumes almost all of our emotional bandwidth.

The experience of these strong emotions (that are typically 'negative' ones, such as anger, frustration, stress, sadness, disappointment, hostility or embarrassment) narrows our awareness. Our focus becomes powerfully centred on the one incident that has precipitated our emotion. Our thoughts are centred on doing whatever it takes to stop the problem that has created the emotion.

Think back to the father who, after watching a scary movie with his daughter, got angry when she delayed going to bed. Her strong emotion (fear) stopped her from thinking rationally. She would not reason or listen. She became more and more upset until she was emotionally flooded. Then, her high emotion was 'caught' by her dad. Because of the discomfort of those emotions, her dad became fixated on doing whatever it took to force a solution. His thinking was, 'My daughter must go to bed and get some sleep. Once she's asleep she won't be afraid and I won't be angry'. His thoughts became narrowed to the point that he saw no alternative solutions to the problem at hand other than to use force to resolve the issue. The 'emotion contagion' meant that two people were emotionally flooded, and no one was listening, understanding or learning.

If we are not mindful parents, we might catch our children's emotions. If our children are angry with us, it can be contagious. We become angry back. And we stop thinking of ways we can work *with* our children. Our anger leads us to work *against* them so that we can get what we want. We may be successful in quelling the emotional uprising in our toddler or teen, but there can be unanticipated costs from responding the way we are naturally equipped to respond.

Contrast the negative with positive emotions. When we feel good (such as when experiencing joy, happiness, contentment, harmony), we can think expansively. We can consider lots of alternatives. We are quite rational. Research has shown that positive emotions lead to wide-ranging thoughts and a mind full of possibilities.[2] When our children are experiencing feelings of sadness, fear or anger, they need us to be in control of our emotions so that we can offer them the understanding they require to work through their feelings. If they can do this, they will quickly begin to feel good again by mirroring our calmness.

Parents talk too much

In communication theory, a person sends a message (in this case verbally) to a listener, who receives it and interprets it correctly. It sounds simple, so why is it sometimes difficult when we sit down with our children or loved ones to talk? Something goes wrong somewhere in the transmission.

Stephen R. Covey, author of *The 7 Habits of Highly Effective People*, tells of an experience he had with a man following a presentation he gave:

> A father once told me, 'I can't understand my kid. He just won't listen to me at all.'
>
> 'Let me restate what you just said,' I replied. 'You don't understand your son because he won't listen to you?'
>
> 'That's right,' he replied.
>
> 'Let me try again,' I said. 'You don't understand your son because *he* won't listen to *you*?'
>
> 'That's what I said,' he impatiently replied.
>
> 'I thought that to understand another person, *you* needed to listen to *him*,' I suggested.
>
> 'Oh!' he said. There was a long pause. 'Oh!' he said again, as the light began to dawn. 'Oh, yeah! But I do understand him. I know what he's going through. I went through the same thing myself. I guess what I don't understand is why he won't listen to me.'[3]

This story perfectly illustrates one of the most significant challenges we face in communicating with our children. As parents, we forget to listen. We think we 'know' what our children are going through, and we try to tell them how to deal with their challenges. The angry father at the start of this chapter would have been able to identify that his daughter was scared. He 'knew' what she was going through. But he only knew it at a cognitive, or intellectual, level. At an emotional level, he showed limited understanding, and his response showed frustration and contempt for her emotions. He understood that she was scared, but he didn't show that he understood. Furthermore, because he felt like he understood her, he just wanted her to listen to him so he could 'fix' her. But our children don't want to be 'fixed'. (Nor do our spouses, mothers-in-law, co-workers or neighbours.) They don't want our lengthy lectures detailing our solutions to their challenges. What our children want is to be understood. They want to *know* that we really do understand what they are struggling with. Then they can feel secure enough to develop *their own* solutions.

To understand our children requires that we listen to them and connect with the emotions they are feeling. This does two miraculous things. First, it fulfils our children's greatest need – that of our emotional availability. Second, it often resolves problems, emotions and challenging behaviour more quickly than our standard, highly emotive responses, without us having to 'fix' things, lecture our children or 'discipline' them.

The bedtime scenario could have played out very differently if the father had connected with, or engaged, his daughter's fear the following way:

> 'Isabela, it sounds as though the movie has frightened you more than we thought. You seem really upset by it.'
>
> Isabela would likely have nodded, recognising the emotions her father was identifying in her. Chances are that having her father acknowledge and identify the serious emotion that she was experiencing would have led to a powerful reduction in those feelings. In this particular scenario, Isabela's father may have needed to do a little more to see his daughter peacefully off to sleep. However, the major objective has already been achieved. Emotions have been brought back to a level where they can be easily regulated and managed, and stress is reduced for both Isabela and her dad. Then they can hug, relax and Dad can softly help his daughter to sleep by singing a song, lying next to her or reading to her.

What is the process? It happens so quickly and easily that it is easy to overlook. All Isabela's dad needed to do initially was to identify and label his daughter's emotions. That's it! Identify the emotion, and then label it. No need for talking. No need for lengthy lectures. No need to even be 'right' or to do any teaching. 'Isabela, you seem really scared and upset by the movie.' Stop there! No more talking. Job done.

Parents talk too much. When our children are experiencing a strong emotion – whether through immaturity, disobedience, stress, fear or otherwise – we tend to dive right in and tell them how to fix things. But our children don't want, or need, our critique. They are unlikely to benefit from our judgement. Our chance to 'fix' them will come later, when things have calmed down. By simply labelling the fear and inviting conversation, we can begin the process of relieving our children of the concerns they feel.

> **Points to ponder**
>
> Think of a time when you were overwhelmed by something in your life and somebody sat with you and just listened as you talked about your feelings. How did their recognition of your feelings affect you? What did it do to the emotions you had been experiencing?
>
> Compare that experience with a time when you were overwhelmed by something in your life and somebody tried to tell you to 'get over' your feelings, or they ignored your feelings. Perhaps they started giving you solutions to your challenges and telling you how to fix the problem. How did their dismissal of your feelings affect you? What did that do to the emotions you were experiencing?

PUTTING IT INTO PRACTICE

Next time your child experiences a big emotion, connect with it. Label it. Then listen. Watch how this process changes the way your child responds to things that are big and frightening.

Will identifying emotions and labelling them 'fix' every emotional situation your children experience? No, of course not. Sometimes our children need lots of time, hugs and a good listening ear. But in the majority of cases, this simple process is enough to start creating calm.

All feelings are OK, and most feelings are normal

Children have lots of big emotions. They are often experiencing things that do not make sense to them. Toddlers watch a parent leave and may not understand that it is only for a brief moment. Children have playground spats with friends that create social distress. Some children experience loneliness. Teenagers feel anger when limits are imposed on them, stymieing their freedom.

In my workshops, I like to ask parents which emotions are OK, and which ones are not. If I ask with just the right intonation and inflection I can usually get the majority of parents to willingly offer that emotions like anger, sadness and fear are undesirable. They don't want their children to feel frightened, upset or mad. Even when parents recognise that these emotions are a normal part of life, many still acknowledge that they would prefer their children not have them. When their children do have these emotions, parents also typically admit that their first priority is to stop the emotion.

Liam was four years old. He had done his best to stand still and quiet in the aisle of the aeroplane, but the anticipation was driving him to distraction. The plane had been on the tarmac for at least five minutes. It had taxied to the terminal. People were standing up to exit the cabin and move into the airport. Liam knew his grandparents were waiting on the other side of the cabin door, but it would not open fast enough for him. Liam was literally jumping up and down on the spot with anticipation. He was dying to catapult himself into his Pop's arms. His movement and occasional shouts that the airline attendants 'Hurry up!' were beginning to embarrass his parents, and cause some discomfort for other passengers.

Liam's mother leaned over and whispered in his ear, 'Liam, you're really excited aren't you? Waiting can be really frustrating can't it? You just wish they'd open up the door so you can see Nan and Pop!'

Liam agreed. He was excited. He didn't want to wait. He wanted his grandparents. But his mum's questions settled the big emotions enough for him to listen.

'Liam, what do we do when we get too excited?'

Liam paused, stared at his mum, and replied, 'Take some big breaths'.

Liam was experiencing the big emotion of excitement. It was flooding his system and he was struggling to regulate himself. Liam's mum could easily have 'caught' the big emotion and gotten excited, or frustrated, with him. It would be easy to be embarrassed by her son's lack of inhibition, and scold him. Instead, she recognised, acknowledged and labelled the emotion Liam was experiencing. Then she invited him to practise something that they had rehearsed before. He took some big breaths, regained control, and was able to wait out the final moments before the aeroplane door was opened and he could run to his grandparents.

When our emotions increase, our behaviour becomes harder to regulate. Our physiology changes as our heart rate and blood pressure build and hormones race around our body. All of these changes can be difficult for adults to handle. It can be almost impossible for children to regulate their emotions, particularly when they are young.

Four-year-old Lily and her two-year-old sister, Ollie, were playing with their toys. A disagreement occurred and Lily screamed, 'I hate you' at Ollie, before pushing her over in a tussle for a toy.

Their mum raced into the room, demanded that Lily apologise, and reprimanded her. 'You don't hate Ollie. You love her. She's your sister. Now say you're sorry.'

At that moment, however, Lily was angry. Being forced to apologise didn't make her feel closer to Ollie. Instead, she resented Ollie, and she was upset with her mum.

If mum had looked after Ollie, and then gone to Lily and said, 'I see you're very upset with Ollie', the response may have been quite different. Lily would have explained what happened.

'Wow, and that made you feel really angry didn't it?'

In a few short moments, Lily would likely have calmed down. Then, teaching would have been able to occur, and it is likely that it would be far more effective once emotions were brought back to within a fairly normal range.

Research indicates that children will be about eight years of age before they can consistently and competently regulate their emotions.[4] Regulating big emotions is a major developmental task of childhood, and there can be challenging times in those eight years for parents. These emotions, however, are a significant part of our lives. We need to feel them, and we also need to be aware of how we act on them. As parents, we often disapprove of our children's emotions. We dismiss their sadness as silly; we are annoyed at their anger; we are frustrated when they are fearful. These responses set off a series of questions in our children's minds that lead to them wondering whether or not they are normal for actually experiencing the emotion. They may think, 'If I'm having this emotion and getting in trouble, perhaps there's something wrong with me. This emotion must not be normal because I keep being told that it is silly or that I shouldn't have it'. The way we respond to our children's emotional state teaches them about whether emotions are appropriate or not. As the renowned psychologist Haim Ginott wrote, 'It is a deep comfort to children to discover that their feelings are a normal part of the human experience'.[5]

Puffer fish parenting

Sometimes we let our emotions get the better of us. Some years ago I read an article that compared some parenting responses to the defence mechanisms of puffer fish.[6] A puffer fish is small and innocent-looking, but if it perceives anything surprising or threatening in its environment, it changes in an instant. By taking on large volumes of air, the fish can puff up to four or five times its original size almost instantly, thereby discouraging others from upsetting it.

When our children experience strong emotions, we can feel disturbed or threatened, and may respond like the puffer fish, blowing up out of all proportion in order to control, manipulate and discourage our children from acting on their emotions around us.

'You did what? I can't believe you would do that! How many times …'

'That is IT! I have had enough!'

Sometimes our puffer fish parenting is a lot more than yelling.

'Go to your room, young lady – and don't come out at all.'

'You stupid idiot! Are you the dumbest six-year-old on the face of the planet?'

Many parents have blown up to such an extent that children have suffered physically. What does a child learn from these outbursts? It is likely that our children will learn that their emotions are wrong. They learn that the big person does not understand them. They may start to feel that there is something wrong with them because of the way that they feel.

Emotional first aid

When our children are experiencing big emotions because of frustration, fear, sadness or anger, the most effective thing that we can do is respond to their distress with emotional first aid. In so doing, we can provide them with the comfort that they need. By being emotionally available and offering our understanding, we are able to reduce the emotional flooding that might otherwise occur, stop the high emotions catching on, acknowledge the emotions that are occurring and not have to talk too much.

This is an example of how emotional first aid works:

> The thud on the floor was enough of a prompt for Heather to start running to her daughter's bedroom. As Heather entered the room and saw Clementine in a heap on the floor, she immediately recognised what had gone wrong. Clementine had been disobedient. She had been told many times that bouncing on the top bunk of her bed was against the rules, and she understood why.
>
> Her mum realised instantly that she had a choice to make. She could lecture Clementine, using all of those lines parents love to recite:
>
> 'How many times have I told you, Clementine? No bouncing on the bed!'
>
> 'You'll get no sympathy from me, young lady. You know better.'
>
> 'If I've told you once, I've told you a thousand times. Don't jump on your bed.'
>
> 'Serves you right. Do as you're told and these things won't happen.'

Had Heather responded in such a way, how would her daughter have felt? Would her emotions have settled? Would she have learned? Do you think that Clementine would have looked up at her mum, calmed down and wisely nodded, 'Gee Mum, you've really taught me an important lesson here. Thanks for helping me see that my judgement was poor, that I should listen to your instructions more closely, and that I may be an impediment to my own safety'. Clementine's mum was wiser than that.

> Heather knew that the learning had already taken place and there was little that she could teach her daughter from this point. She knelt beside her and held her. Then Heather provided some *emotional first aid*.
>
> 'Clementine, we heard you crying. You must be hurt.' Heather offered her comfort. 'Would you like a cuddle?' She offered her assistance. 'Where does it hurt? Do you need anything?' These responses calmed Clementine quickly. Clementine's emotions were identified and labelled.
>
> Some time after Clementine's emotions were under control, her mum was able to ask her calmly, 'Clemmie, what did you learn from what just happened?'
>
> She did not want to respond. 'You're a little embarrassed, aren't you?'
>
> Again her mum identified her emotions. Clementine was then able to acknowledge she had done the wrong thing, and identify how she might be more careful in future.

When Clementine's mum demonstrated that she understood how she felt, and explicitly labelled her emotions, Clementine felt emotionally safe and understood. This is emotional first aid. It is not usually the end of the process – just as physical first aid is not usually the end of repairing a physical wound – but it is a necessary and important first step.

Failing to provide emotional first aid has obvious short-term consequences. Our children don't calm down, but instead feel foolish, angry, alienated and incapable of regulating their apparently 'abnormal' behaviour. But long-term consequences can be even worse. Our relationships with our children can be damaged from deep wounds caused by anger. Our children may model our behaviour with younger siblings. As teens, they may rebel more readily. And ultimately, as parents they are likely to repeat the cycle.

Points to ponder

Think of an experience today when someone was experiencing a big emotion. Perhaps it was your children, your boss or even your spouse.

- Was your child (or other person) highly emotive? Was it likely that they were emotionally flooded?
- Did you catch their emotion, or were you able to be emotionally available enough – mindful enough – to simply be present?
- Did you talk too much? Or were you able to provide emotional first aid by labelling the emotion they were feeling, and then listening with understanding?

Review the experience and think of the words you might have said to show understanding, provide emotional first aid and prevent the emotions from either flooding the person, or becoming contagious. How would you do it better next time?

The principles outlined in this chapter are some of the most challenging habits we can implement in our relationships. Really *understanding* another person requires a willingness to be humble and recognise that we do not have all the answers. It requires us to look into the hearts of our children and try to imagine exactly what it must be like for them. As parents, this can be a struggle. When our child is experiencing an emotion, we often believe that we understand its cause and its solution and then we try to fix the problem. But this is not what our children need. They just need us to show them that we understand the emotion, and then we can support them as *they* work on fixing the problem.

Ways of communicating that show understanding

It is worth practising statements that diffuse big emotions, demonstrate understanding and offer emotional first aid so that we can fall back on them quickly and effortlessly when they are needed. The first thing that we can do to show we understand, and to provide the first aid that is so necessary, is to acknowledge the feelings our children are having. Specifically identifying the emotion and giving it a label will make the emotion OK. When our children know what they are feeling has a name, they seem to regulate themselves better, and work through the emotion. We might say to our children, 'You seem very concerned (upset, hurt, afraid, confused, distracted, etc.)', or 'You feel strongly about this'.

Once we have labelled the emotion, it can be useful to invite further discussion, but in a gentle way. The following statement is a soft, understanding way of doing this: 'I want to understand what you're feeling. Will you tell me a little more?' Alternatively, it might be helpful to ask, 'Would you like to share how you're feeling?' Such questions allow children to decide whether or not to talk, and if they are willing to do so, they can decide how much to share.

If a successful dialogue commences, it is important to show understanding. Rather than becoming autobiographical, we can reflect what we are hearing: 'I wish I could understand exactly what you're feeling'; 'I can tell that what you're going through is really difficult'. Being there through the emotion and applying emotional first aid to hurt feelings will see those emotions diminish reasonably quickly in most circumstances. Such an approach shows understanding.

There will be some times when our children say things to us without any great emotion, but with some concern.

Seven-year-old Ella's aunt was getting married. Ella asked her mother whether her aunt would be having flower girls at her wedding. Her mum announced that there were no plans for flower girls. Ella seemed satisfied.

A week before the wedding, a change to the plans was discussed. Ella's aunt wanted two flower girls, but they were to be the youngest two of her seven nieces. Ella was not one of them. Again Ella went to her mum. This time she wanted to know why there were two flower girls.

Ella's mum could have explained all of the reasons why the two little girls had been chosen over Ella. But she recognised the emotion Ella was experiencing. She said, 'Ella, you wish you could be one of your aunt's flower girls, don't you.' Ella nodded. 'It would make you feel very important, wouldn't it?' More confirmation from Ella. Then Ella's mum hugged Ella, assured her of her love and importance, and let the issue go. Ella was satisfied. She felt understood. She had received the emotional first aid she needed. Her mum had said very little, but everything was alright.

It is up to us to show that we see things from the perspective of our children. When we do this they will calm down more quickly. We can communicate our understanding in any number of different ways. All that matters is that our children recognise that we do *really* understand their feelings. We don't have to agree with them. We don't have to give them what it is that they are after. All it means is that we show them that we see things the way that they see them.

Reality check

Trying to apply emotional first aid will not always work out. Sometimes a situation is too highly charged, or too personal for our children to work through with us.

I arrived home from work on a particular afternoon and my eldest daughter, almost a teenager, was terribly upset. She was hurting her sisters, being disrespectful to her mother and stubbornly refusing to carry out any of her responsibilities. What were my options?

I chose to be understanding. I removed myself from the situation and invited my daughter to come with me. She did not want to, but reluctantly complied. I invited her to take a few minutes in her room to calm down because I could tell that it had not been a good afternoon. We both went to

»

our rooms to settle our emotions, and then I went to spend time with her.

'You're feeling pretty lousy.'

I got no response. I tried again. 'You don't really want to talk with me, do you? You'd rather just be left alone.'

Still no response. At this point I acknowledged that if that was how she felt, I would leave her for now, and come back to see if she felt like talking a little later. I also told her she was free to stay in her room or leave it, but that if she returned to the family, she knew what was expected of her.

Again, no response.

Some time later, I returned. We repeated the process with the same outcome. The same thing happened on my next attempt to talk with her. Dinner was served and she refused to join us. All the while, I demonstrated that I understood that she was feeling judged, upset, annoyed by her sisters, mad that she couldn't choose to do what she wanted and so on.

Eventually she ate dinner, alone, and returned to her room. I tried one more time. I was met with more silence. I again affirmed that I understood how she felt, and that if she felt like talking about it in the morning we could do that.

The next morning there was no further progress. I restated our family's rules for getting along, asked her to confirm that she knew what was expected and reassured her that if she wished to talk, I was available.

There was no speedy resolution. But there were no tantrums. There was no aggression or frustration. There was no power struggle. After my daughter had worked through her issues, she happily and willingly rejoined our family activities. She did so knowing her feelings had been respected, and that she was participating of her own free will and choice.

A cynic might say, 'What was the point?' The point is that when we show understanding, we salvage a relationship from what might otherwise become a mess. We treat our children like humans, respect them and ensure they recognise that we value them. We put the relationship above the behaviours and emotions that are jeopardising it.

Sometimes emotional first aid will not achieve the goal of you and your children coming to a speedy and simple resolution. But, if you have shown your children that you value them, have demonstrated a sound understanding of their emotions and can clearly state that you will put the relationship first, then something just as important will have been achieved. Emotional availability and parental responsiveness through understanding are the two key building blocks of a strong relationship between parent and child. Not everything can be resolved, particularly when emotions run high. But with patience, a willingness to look into another person's heart and the capacity to show understanding, relationships will be stronger, and families will be happier.

Notes

1   C Stead, *The man who loved children*, The Miegunyah Press, Melbourne, 2011. Afterword by Randall Jarrell.
2   BL Fredrickson & LE Kurtz, 'Cultivating positive emotions to enhance human flourishing', in SI Donaldson, M Csikszentmihalyi & J Nakamura (eds), *Applied positive psychology: improving everyday life, health, schools, work, and society*, Routledge, New York, 2011, pp. 35–48.
3   SR Covey, *The 7 habits of highly effective people*, Free Press, New York, 2004, p. 239.
4   CC Peterson, *Looking forward through the lifespan: developmental psychology*, 5th edn, Pearson Education, Sydney, 2009.
5   H Ginnott, A Ginott & HW Goddard, *Between parent and child: the bestselling classic that revolutionized parent–child communication*, revised and updated, Three Rivers Press, New York, 2003, p. 21.
6   SE Brotherson, 'Anger, puffer fish parenting and love', *Meridian Magazine*, 30 October 2003.

Discipline: Teaching Children Good Ways to Act

3

'The essence of discipline is to teach good ways to act'
Dr H Wallace Goddard[1]

It is ironic that we use disciplinary strategies that are so unkind towards those whom we love so deeply. We seem to expect perfection in our children, forgetting our own humanity and the many mistakes and learning experiences we went through as children and are still going through as parents. If we can be emotionally available to our children and understand their feelings, we can begin to discipline more effectively.

Unfortunately the discipline most parents use is punitive in nature. That is, it's about punishing our children for doing the 'wrong' thing. Our aim is to 'teach them a lesson'. But these methods do not work, and they rupture our relationships with our children. They may achieve short-term compliance, but they do not teach our children the lessons we need them to learn. Picture this situation:

> You are at a family gathering when you notice that all of your children, and everyone else's children, are gone. You discover that an uncle has taken all twenty or so children to the beach – about a 500 metre walk from the house the function is being held at. It is the middle of winter.
>
> You walk to the beach to make sure that everything is OK and discover the uncle and the children making their way back to the party ... dripping wet, covered in sand and shivering with cold! Well, the children are wet,
>
> »

sandy and cold. Their uncle – the responsible adult who took them – is still dry and smiling.

He tells you that everyone was playing on the sand when one of the children decided to wade into the water. The other children all followed. He asked them to come away from the water, but as they did so one of them fell over. This child got wet, and several others got wet from the splash of the child falling in. Within seconds other children copied the idea, 'accidentally' tripping and falling into the water. Moments later the adult in charge could no longer prevent the children from swimming, so he let them splash, play and swim, fully clothed until they'd had enough.

You live an hour or more away. You have no spare clothes for your children. It's freezing cold, and your children are all 'old enough to know better'.

How would you react? Would you get angry at the grown-up for letting it happen? Or would you decide that your children ought to be 'disciplined' because of their inappropriate behaviour?

Did the children actually do anything 'wrong'? Not really. Was it foolish? Inconvenient? Perhaps. But as a seven-year-old, didn't you love to play in the water?

As grown-ups we often choose to 'discipline' our children over things that are not necessarily morally wrong, but are more 'inconvenient'. And the more I have thought about this, the more I have become convinced that in the majority of cases (though not always), we get annoyed, upset or angry at our children for the way they inconvenience our lives more than we get upset with them for doing the 'wrong' thing.

Points to ponder

- Stop and think about the last few times you were irritated by your child's activities. Were those activities morally wrong? Or were they simply inconvenient and annoying?

Sometimes the things that our children do that are inconvenient *do* need to be corrected. Children *do* need to learn that colouring in the cream-coloured couch with red finger paint (as my three-year-old Annie did one afternoon) is wrong. (I said to Annie, 'Wow, the couch is colourful now!' Annie looked proud of herself. I then asked her if couches were for painting.

She looked a little less proud. I suggested we do more painting together … on the card stock. She smiled again. Then, as she painted I was able to teach her the 'paint rules'.) But our teaching, whether for moral situations or inconvenient behaviours, need not be punitive.

This chapter cannot possibly deal with all of the challenging behaviours and situations that you will face. Nor can it provide a complete review of all the disciplinary practices that may be useful for you in your family. Instead, I will focus on a few discipline mistakes parents make, and provide a handful of discipline tips that you should be able to implement immediately in your family.

When we know what discipline means, we 'discipline' differently

It seems as though every parent wants to know how to 'control' their children, 'manage their behaviour' and 'make' their children do as they should. Each of these euphemisms for discipline misses the point of what discipline really is. As a result, we often do things that are not necessarily helpful when we need to discipline our children.

One evening, my family was enjoying dinner at the home of some friends. Between us and our friends we had nine children under the age of eleven. It was a noisy, busy affair. Nevertheless, the evening was completely wonderful until …

The youngest son of our friends was named Ryan. Ryan, aged two, decided he had eaten enough of his chicken satay. He picked up his fork, looked at his five-year-old brother, Jacob, and stabbed him in the face with the fork.

Everyone saw it. And while Jacob groped at his forehead and screamed in pain, Ryan looked quite proud of himself.

The boys' father reacted swiftly, jumping to his feet and taking Ryan from the room. A few seconds later he came back into the room and stared at me, before demanding, 'You're the parenting expert. What am I supposed to do now?'

My friend's natural reaction had been fairly normal. He was concerned for the welfare of one child, and angry at another child for doing something 'naughty'. He had yelled at his two-year-old and enforced a 'time-out'. Now he wanted to find out if that was what he should have done, or if there was something better that may have helped to teach his son how to behave.

Let me be clear about this: Ryan's behaviour was not just inconvenient. It was wrong. So discipline was needed. But when it comes to discipline, our natural reactions often fail to effectively do any 'disciplining' at all. Time-out, spanking, star charts and rewards may stop challenging behaviour in the moment, but only because we are present to be the police. Our children's reasons for compliance are not internalised. Instead, they are doing as we asked because we are managing their behaviour. Marshall Rosenberg clarifies:

> Two questions help us see why we are unlikely to get what we want by using punishment … The first question is: 'What do I want this person to do that's different from what he or she is currently doing?' If we ask only this first question, punishment may seem effective, because the threat or exercise of punitive force may well influence someone's behavior. However, with the second question, it becomes evident that punishment isn't likely to work: 'What do I want this person's reasons to be for doing what I'm asking?'[2]

The purpose of discipline is to *teach* good ways to act. Ideally, our discipline will be centred on training our children, instructing them and helping them learn to exercise self-control. Our discipline will be about guidance rather than coercion. True discipline helps a child discover his or her own reason for making good choices, rather than forcing them to 'behave' out of fear or for the promise of a goodie. True discipline takes the management of our children's behaviour out of our hands and puts it into *theirs*.

Before I describe some of the ideal strategies for discipline, I think it is important to review some of the reasons that our more common strategies – the punitive methods that aim to make a child pay a penalty for their behaviour – do not work.

Smacking

Studies show that well over 90% of parents hit their children under the age of four regularly, with nearly 60% acknowledging they smack their 5–9-year-old children.[3] My research, involving a comprehensive study of 509 parents, suggests that at least 65% of Australian mums and dads smack their children.[4] While most parents acknowledge that smacking is not ideal, it seems the vast majority of parents still hit their kids. There are four main arguments against smacking:

- Violence breeds violence. When parents use physical force to 'manage behaviour', they model coercion as acceptable and appropriate for problem solving. Research has found that children who were spanked more than twice a month were 50% more likely to develop aggressive behaviours than those who weren't spanked at all. These bullying behaviours included getting into fights, being mean to others and destroying toys and property.[5]
- There is strong evidence that smacking children reduces their IQ. Those who think smacking is fine often say, 'My father smacked me and it never did me any harm'. This illogical line of reasoning assumes that smacking will make a person a sociopath, and while this is an unlikely extreme, recent research has indicated stress and anxiety (due to fear of punishment) may slow children's cognitive development. The punishment does not have to be severe to have an impact; however children who receive severe corporal punishment have been shown to possess significantly less grey matter than children who do not receive such treatment. This means fewer neurons that can aid in development and intelligence.[6]
- Some say they smack because 'you can't reason with a toddler or small child'. If this argument is followed to its natural and logical end, carers should be able to physically punish adults with intellectual disabilities or dementia. The very fact that toddlers do not have sufficient reasoning skills suggests that they need more, and not less, protection.
- Smacking is simply not effective for discipline. If smacking were really effective, it would stop the challenging behaviour. While there is an immediate benefit for the parent who smacks (where the child does actually stop the challenging behaviour), it only lasts briefly. The behaviour inevitably returns, but it usually does so more insidiously. Smacking and the threat of physical punishment push the behaviour underground, turning our children into subversive, but careful, dissidents.

Some people will still argue that a 'loving tap' does not hurt a child – but a smack that does not hurt can be laughed off or ignored. It is pointless and will not have its intended effect. The point of hitting is to affirm power, be dominant and control a child by showing her who is boss. Australian researchers Terry Dobbs and Judith Duncan illuminate the impact of these motivations on children in a study they conducted.

When children were asked to describe smacking, they said, 'It hurts and it makes you cry'. In this response is a physical pain and also an emotional pain. Children further articulated this by acknowledging that smacking makes them 'feel sad'.

- Children indicated that they were regularly smacked for hurting others. The irony is striking.
- The children studied did not perceive the 'loving taps' as gentle. Instead, they consistently defined them as a 'hard hit' or a 'very hard hit'.
- Parents often claim to be in complete control while administering the 'tap', yet the children studied perceived that parents only smacked when angry, whether they were or not. It is these perceptions that are important.
- All the children in the study felt that it was not OK to smack.[7]

In summary, research abundantly demonstrates that not only does smacking have the potential to physically hurt children, it also:

- models aggression and violence
- fails to teach communication
- makes 'discipline' (i.e. punishment) about power
- fails to teach empathy and perspective
- forces unacceptable behaviour underground
- reduces social competence and ability to make friends
- promotes bullying
- reduces children's self esteem.

Remember, too, that punishment loses its effectiveness over time. Smacking may work with three-year-olds (I'd argue it doesn't) but have you ever tried to smack a 14-year-old?

Time-out

One of the most popular 'discipline' methods parents employ is the 'time-out'. This typically consists of responding to children's challenging behaviour with the direction that they sit somewhere boring and free of distractions for a set amount of time to think about what was wrong with their behaviour. After that period of time, children will supposedly be remorseful and will also have learned their lesson. But does it really teach them anything?

Time-out is really a politically correct euphemism for what Alfie Kohn more appropriately identifies as 'forcible isolation'.[8] In real terms, time-out involves a person of higher power using that power to hand down a sentence of solitary confinement to an essentially powerless child. Time-out is *love withdrawal*. Here's a snapshot of what researchers have discovered about children who experience love withdrawal via the experience of time-out:

- Children become distressed when their parents threaten to leave them, particularly when the threat is associated with a child's challenging behaviour.
- Children will become highly compliant with a parent's requests at the threat of love withdrawal.
- Time-out may be more emotionally devastating than other punishments despite there being no physical or material threat, because it poses the ultimate threat of abandonment or separation. The parent may know when it will end but the very young child is totally dependent.
- The child who is repeatedly given time-out is far more likely to experience anxiety about love from their parents.
- Time-out leaves kids in greater emotional distress for longer periods than does smacking.
- Kids who experience love withdrawal through the use of time-out and/or threats of abandonment (even for short periods) typically have lower self-esteem, poorer emotional health and are prone to increased challenging behaviour than children who do not experience love withdrawal.[9]

Of course, a multitude of parenting experts claim that time-out is the most effective behaviour management strategy there is. In other words, time-out 'works'. But what does it work to do? And more importantly, what does it teach children?

Time-out is a power-based discipline. The power we have as parents is used to make a child suffer to change their behaviour. This teaches children that the big person is always right, and even if the big person isn't right, he or she can make the smaller person do unpleasant things.

Time-out teaches kids that their emotions and behaviours aren't acceptable. Sometimes behaviour is unacceptable and needs to be regulated. The same goes for emotions, but forced time-out is not an effective way to help a child to do this.

Time-out creates anxiety, and teaches children that a parent's love is conditional. This impacts negatively on the relationship between parent and child, and also on the feelings of worth the child experiences.

Time-out has some merit when used in one of the two following ways:

- First, by giving ourselves time-out when we become frustrated, we are better able to control our responses to our children's challenging behaviour. Children also get the message that we are upset when we remove ourselves and they often remedy their behaviour without our intervention.

- Second, when we give our children the option to go some place of their choosing so they can work through their emotions, we respect their autonomy. The time-out is chosen, rather than being banishment.

Time-out and smacking are the two most common punishments that children receive in the name of 'discipline'. But they don't really teach our children anything we want them to learn. The problem with these forms of discipline is that they involve power, rather than love. They involve us *doing things to* our children, rather than working *with* them. Whenever we focus on doing things to our children we are going for low skill, low effort, little time and little introspection techniques that never really teach our children anything other than to avoid mum and dad if there's a problem.

Working with your children, not doing things to your children

Several years ago I came across a story that perfectly illustrates the difference between doing things to someone, and working with someone.

A man who had never ridden a horse married a woman who loved horses. Shortly after their wedding, while visiting a farm, he told his new wife that he was going to go outside to the recently-born colt and teach it to be 'led'. He assumed it would be simple. He would attach a rope to the colt's halter, pull gently on it, and as he walked, he presumed that the colt would follow. He was bigger and smarter than the colt, and he assured his wife he would get the job done in no time.

The man sauntered down to the paddock with a lead rope. He attached it to the colt's halter. Then he turned, took two steps until the slack was taken from the rope, and came to an unexpected, and sudden, stop. The colt refused to move. The man pulled the rope harder, expecting that the force would motivate the colt to move. Instead, the colt resisted, pulling back against the man with equal force. Then the man pulled the colt much harder. The colt fell over.

After a moment, the colt stood up again, so the man made a second attempt to coerce the colt into walking with him. He was determined to teach this colt to be led! He pulled. The colt returned to its place on the ground.

It stood once again. He pulled hard once again. It rolled to the ground once again. After repeating this pattern several times, the man acknowledged that it had taken him around five minutes to teach the colt to fall over. All he had to do was stand in front of it, tug on the rope and the colt would willingly fall to the ground.

The man's bemused wife had followed him into the paddock and after watching for several minutes, made a suggestion borne of experience with horses.

'Why don't you stand beside the colt rather than standing in front of it? And instead of pulling the rope, perhaps you could wrap the rope gently across the back of its neck and simply walk alongside it.'

'I'm in charge, and it needs to do as I say', the man argued. After successfully putting the colt on the ground again, the man reluctantly agreed to try his wife's method. To his chagrin, his wife's suggestion worked.

As parents, we often fall into the same trap as this new husband. We weigh more than our children. We know more than our children. And often we assume that all we need to do is 'pull on the lead rope' and sooner or later our children will follow. You don't have to have been a parent for very long to realise that children consistently act like the colt in the story. They resist our efforts to lead them. And when they do so, we have a decision to make. The default position for most parents is to start to pull harder on the rope – that is, to demand, force or coerce our children to follow. We *do things to* our children to discipline (or teach) them. We act as an external force. They *react* to us.

There are a number of problems with this. First, it models coercion. Kids grow up thinking the big person always wins. Children who grow up in homes where their parents consistently 'throw their weight around' are likely to have lower feelings of self-worth than other kids. Compared with children whose parents are less coercive, they are also more likely to become bullies themselves, throwing their weight around the schoolyard.

Second, it turns us into the police. We're constantly trying to catch our kids out. And they start to get sneaky. When we threaten and coerce our children, using phrases like, 'Don't you ever let me catch you doing that again', our children respond, 'OK, you won't catch me doing that again'. Their behaviour becomes subversive, hidden, underhanded and devious.

Third, our teaching is often lost in the flood of emotions our children fear as they await their punishment, and we become impotent guides in our children's lives. Rather than listening to our wisdom, our children become fearful of the 'consequences' they're about to receive. As such, anything useful we may have been about to say is lost in the powerful emotions of fear, guilt, shame and sadness our child feels as we do things to them to teach them.

Fourth, and most important, our children do not internalise correct ways of behaving. Instead, they act out of fear or to please us. Once the external force is no longer present, they no longer feel compelled to do the right thing.

When we *work with* our children, something different happens. Our children have an opportunity to see how challenges can be dealt with in a mature, non-coercive way. There is a lot less emotion, and we don't have to continually police our children. They internalise the behaviours, limits and lessons we wish them to learn because *they* are the ones doing the talking and thinking – not us.

We can command, coerce and control all we like as parents and, because we're bigger, we'll generally win. But there comes a time when such strategies cease to be effective. By the time a child is around twelve years old, our use of force and coercion becomes ineffective. Trying to learn new strategies becomes more difficult due to our ingrained patterns of behaviour, and our children will be highly resistant to a more democratic way of working through challenges.

Further, by the time our children are around twelve, we have more or less used up our critical years of influence. The best part of our teaching is essentially completed. That is not to say that we will not have many more teaching opportunities with our children throughout their adolescent years. But the extent of our influence is decreased. Our adolescent children rely on us less, listen to us less and learn from us less.

There are strategies and skills we can develop that will teach our children good ways to act without us needing to use coercion or punitive methods that force compliance. These strategies include having an understanding of our children's development; induction; perspective taking; using gentle reminders; and knowing when to discipline and when to let our children learn for themselves, and they will be discussed in turn below.

Understand your child's development

My family was attending a church service one Sunday and my two-year-old daughter was struggling to sit quietly for the extended period of time. I did what most young dads might do in similar circumstances. Through gritted teeth and with a faux smile in case someone could see me, I whispered, 'Chanel, if you don't sit still and quiet, I'm going to take you outside and smack your bottom'.

I used a 'doing to' approach to manage my daughter's behaviour. And the threat seemed to work. Chanel sat up straight, eyes front. She looked hurt, but she got the message.

About three minutes later Chanel recommenced her disruptive wriggling. Then she looked up at me with big, sad eyes. When I met her gaze she asked, 'Daddy, will you take me outside and smack my bottom?'

I was not particularly well attuned to the capacity of a two-year-old to sit still for seventy minutes during a sermon. Many adults can't even manage it! By understanding the extent of our children's development, we are better able to understand the reasoning behind both their 'inconvenient' and 'wrong' behaviours, and respond with more effective teaching. It may have been useful for me to take Chanel for a walk and ask her why we were at church and what types of behaviours were expected. Perhaps, by understanding that it is asking a lot for a two-year-old child to sit still for that long, I might have spoken to her about remaining quiet, and then provided her with coloured pencils and a book to draw in.

When dealing with Ryan, the toddler who stabbed his brother in the face with a fork at the beginning of this chapter, the best discipline would occur within an understanding of his development. Toddlers are curious experimenters. They want to know how throwing works. They are curious about how hitting things feels. They love repetition, experimenting and developing an understanding of cause and effect. They don't fully comprehend the consequences of their behaviour. They are also extremely limited in their ability to communicate and deal with emotions, challenging situations, general tiredness or hunger. Throwing, stabbing or hitting can give toddlers a sense of control, which may be quite fun for them.

It is important to recognise that sometimes children will intentionally do things that are harmful or inappropriate. Ryan may find it deliciously enticing to stab his brother's face with a fork. The response he got the first time may be just what he wants more of. These challenging behaviours require ongoing teaching. I suggested several of the ideas in this chapter to Ryan's dad. They included understanding Ryan's development, induction (see p. 51) and perspective taking (see p. 54). Though Ryan may be too young to fully comprehend the consequences of his actions, by practising effective discipline habits early, Ryan and his parents (and his brother) will learn good ways to act more quickly than via punitive means.

Go through the following list of items and work out what you think would be an appropriate age for your child to be able to do each of these things.

a) Try to write their name
b) Lift their head and chest when lying on their stomach
c) Put on shoes (not tie laces)
d) Pedal a tricycle
e) Regulate/have control over their emotions
f) Open doors, drawers and everything else
g) Follow multiple commands (e.g. get changed, wash hands, come and eat dinner)
h) Smile when smiled at
i) Brush teeth competently
j) Understand how other people are feeling

k)   Know if they are a boy or a girl
l)   Use the toilet competently
m) Identify several body parts
n)   Walk with one hand held

Answers: a) 4 years; b) 3 months; c) 3 years; d) 3 years; e) 8 years; f) 2 years; g) 6 years;
h) 4 weeks; i) 5 years; j) 5 years; k) 3 years; l) 3.5 years; m) 2 years; n) 1 year.

When we remember that they're just babies, we tend to approach the concept of disciplining and setting limits for our children a little more compassionately. Rather than doing things to them for 'inappropriate behaviour', we recall that their behaviour is actually entirely appropriate. It's what kids at that developmental level do. But just because the behaviour is developmentally appropriate does not make it acceptable. So we begin the process of induction, to teach our children what is acceptable and what is not.

Induction

My father owns a furniture moving company. During my studies, I spent many years working part-time, sweating in the back of a truck lifting fridges, lounge suites and even pianos.

On one job I was asked to assist one of dad's men, Ewen, to move a large piano. Both of us had shifted many pianos, but neither of us had ever been 'in charge' when the pianos had been moved. We had always been the 'offsider', following the instructions of the driver on the job. Nevertheless, we approached the piano with confidence. We lifted the 250 kilogram instrument onto the four-wheeled piano trolley and pushed it to the board leading out of the truck.

I was standing on the board, acting as the brake for the piano, which was more than triple my weight. It was my job to push against it to slow its descent down the ramp. The first two wheels rolled out of the side door of the truck and onto the ramp. I extended my arms to push against the piano, readying myself for the next two wheels to roll over the edge of the truck and down the ramp to the road.

»

The next two wheels were edged onto the ramp as Ewen pulled the piano against gravity, trying to help me slow the trolley. With all four wheels on the ramp, the descent began. It will be no surprise to learn that we lost control of the piano within a second. My extended arms folded like an accordion as the piano accelerated. Ewen pulled against it with all of his might but could not stop it, and he was forced to let go. There was nothing left for me to do but dive.

As I landed on the road and rolled away from the truck, I heard the piano crash off the ramp. It bounced onto the road and rolled straight onto the bottom half of my body, crushing me beneath it. Ewen grabbed a corner of it and lifted it enough for me to drag myself out from underneath. Then, bleeding and limping, I began to help Ewen pick up the hundreds of pieces of shattered piano from the middle of the road.

There were two critical things Ewen and I did wrong in moving this piano. First, a ramp should always be set up to have the shallowest gradient possible. This usually means it should come out of the back of a truck and not the side. And second, the person acting as 'brake' should place their shoulder firmly against the piano to slow it down. Arms can bend (as mine did), whereas shoulders are much more stable with less give.

We had done it the right way dozens of times before, but only because someone else had been calling the shots. We simply didn't know how to do it the right way on our own.

What has this got to do with parenting? Research has shown that *induction* is one of the most effective ways in helping children internalise moral behaviour.[10]

In every role we take on, there are rules for how that role should be carried out. We are usually inducted at work, when we receive training in how things should be done and what behaviours are acceptable. Children need to be inducted as well. Induction is the process of explicitly stating what our expectations are so our children have been taught.

A mother was searching frantically for her toddler. After several minutes of calling his name and looking in every room, she peered through the lounge room window and saw him playing out on the corner, next to the road. She raced outside and scolded him, 'How many times have I told you not to play near the corner?'

He replied, 'What's a corner, Mummy?'

As parents, we assume our children understand the 'rules'. We think they know how to act. Often we may be right, but it is interesting just how regularly we can be wrong. Our children don't always understand the limits we impose, even if they've complied with the limit dozens of times before, and even if we have told them more than once.

A wise teacher once told me that the people who do the best learning are the ones whose mouths are moving. If all of our induction revolves around what we are saying, our children will eventually stop listening. Rather than us doing all of the teaching, the best form of induction occurs when we ask questions. This encourages children to explain what they understand. We can have them describe a rule and the reasons for it. Then, if there are gaps in their understanding we can invite them to think of other answers. This gives them credit for having the capacity to figure things out. And it helps our children develop the answers for themselves rather than consistently being told.

For older children, we may consider involving them in the limit setting process, by providing information relevant to the issue and asking them what they feel is appropriate. When they set the limits, they police themselves.

Points to ponder

Think about the last time you had to discipline one of your children. How well did your child understand what was expected? Who did all the talking? The next opportunity you get, revisit that 'disciplinary moment' with your child.

- Ask them to talk about why they were requiring some 'teaching'.
- Have them explain the rule relevant to the situation.
- Invite them to discuss why it matters, who it affects and how.
- Then observe the degree to which they remain compliant.

Perspective taking

My two eldest children were fighting. Chanel was five years old and Abbie was two. Abbie came to me, sobbing.

'What happened?' I asked. Abbie, choking on air between each sob, blurted out that Chanel had hit her.

'Chanel, come here!' I called. As she entered the room defiantly, I asked, 'What happened to Abbie?'

The response was predictable. 'I don't know. She just started crying. I didn't do anything.'

I should have known better than to ask a question I knew the answer to. Now Chanel was about to be in trouble for hitting, and for lying. Abbie began crying louder, shaking her head, and pointing an accusing finger at Chanel.

'Chanel, I want to do a little experiment with you. I want you to pretend you are Abbie, OK? Now, Abbie, what did Chanel do to you?'

Chanel was quiet for a moment, looked down at the ground, and sheepishly replied, 'She hit me'.

Perspective taking is a powerful disciplinary tool that offers teaching experiences to our children and to us, as grown-ups. The idea developed from Jean Piaget's work in the early 1940s. Piaget is one of the fathers of developmental psychology, and his work has influenced child researchers for nearly a century.[11]

Piaget developed a task to measure children's spatial ability, called the 'Three Mountains Task'. In the task, a child faced a display of three model mountains. After they had walked around the display and seen it clearly from all perspectives, a doll was placed at different viewpoints around the display. Then a researcher would invite the child to look at a series of photographs and identify the photograph that best illustrated what the doll could see. The child, in other words, was being asked to take the perspective of the doll, and see things the way the doll saw them.

Up until around the age of four years, most children struggled to differentiate between what they could see from their own viewpoint, and what the doll could see from an alternative position. The child was too egocentric. But from around the age of five years, children were fairly accurately able to take the perspective of the doll and describe what it could 'see', regardless of where the child may have been situated in relation to the model of the mountains.

This research has led to hundreds of studies that have examined what children can perceive. From around the age of four, most children are able to identify the visual perceptions of another person with reasonable accuracy. They are also able to recognise and perceive the way another person is feeling, and even begin to construct a reason the person may feel the way she does.

When Ryan stabbed Jacob with his fork, he was using his newfound ability to purposefully do things; he was experimenting with 'cause and effect'. But had his father asked him how the stabbing made Jacob feel, Ryan may have struggled to effectively perceive how his actions had hurt his brother. His dad needed to explicitly teach this to him.

I explained to Ryan's dad that Ryan could describe what happened, but may not understand it. Asking questions and helping Ryan understand the rules about forks, food and people's faces was the best way to teach Ryan.

Chanel, at the age of five, however, was able to identify Abbie's perception. She was able to discuss with me how Abbie felt about what she had done to her. And she knew how it made me, as her father, feel.

Perspective taking is a disciplinary process that involves time and understanding. We need to be emotionally available to our children. We need to tread gently, particularly when emotions are raw. Sometimes children do not want to take the perspective of another person. They may be too angry, embarrassed or upset. They often need us to recognise and label those emotions so they feel understood. Then we can begin to teach them good ways to act. Not all children respond immediately to our efforts to see another's perspective. Often they are hurt or have taken offence. They are unhappy, and so they are less inclined to consider another's point of view. But perspective taking is the most powerful way for a child to be disciplined. When we use it, it softens our approach to them, which means that emotions will be lower, and learning is more likely to occur. When they use it to understand how their actions are affecting others, it can shed an enormous amount of light on things for them. It is the process that ensures that learning is internalised.

> **Points to ponder**
> Think about some of the challenges you are having with your child. Think
> of the kinds of questions you can ask that will help your child understand
> things from beyond their own egocentric point of view.
>   Note: Be careful that perspective taking does not become manipulation
> or a guilt trip.

Gentle reminders

A wonderful parenting researcher, writer and speaker, Professor H. Wallace
Goddard, relates the following story:

> I was standing in my neighbour's garage, talking, when my neighbour's
> young boy (aged around five or six) rode his bike into the garage, dropped
> it on the floor, and raced out to continue playing. The man erupted; 'Get
> back here now!'
>   As his son sheepishly returned, the man lifted the boy up over his head
> and, while shaking him suspended two metres off the ground, shouted
> 'How many times do I have to tell you? Put your bike away in the bike rack!
> Stand it up! Look after your things!'
>   After his tirade, the man then half-shouted at his son, 'I love you'.[12]

Goddard asks two poignant questions in relation to this situation. First,
what did the boy learn? And second, was it anything to do with how much
he was 'loved'?

It is unlikely that the little boy, while flailing above his father's head,
thought to himself, 'You know, Dad, you're right, I need to be a lot more
responsible … but at least I know you love me'. The father was trying to
teach his son to put his bike away properly. If achieving compliance is the
metric, his strategy 'worked'. But if raising a son who feels loved, can deal
effectively with challenging situations and internalises good ways to act is
the definition of our discipline working, then this scenario leaves a lot to
be desired. It is likely that the son learned that he is irresponsible, and that
his dad is scary.

There may be another way. Using a gentle reminder, this father
would have called after his son and then said three simple words: 'Your

bike, please'. Would that work? I suspect that this little boy would have responded with a quick apology, and a scampering run back into the garage to remedy the problem.

In my workshops, parent after parent has thanked me for this simple strategy. Parents remain calm. Children think for themselves. Here are the steps for using gentle reminders in your home:

1 Call the person by name.
2 Look at them and quietly remind them of the issue. The fewer words you use the better. Two is ideal. For example, 'Your bedroom', 'Your stinky socks', 'The dishes', and so on.
3 Say please, and smile kindly.

Would that improve the atmosphere in your home? Would that increase the happiness in your family? Would that be a way of modelling behaviour that you'd like to see replicated?

Some parents ask me what happens when immediate compliance is not achieved. My response is usually that it might help to do it again, but this time, ensure you really have their attention. You may have to use the reminder more than once for the same thing – even adults get forgetful, lazy or busy. Sometimes there are bigger issues that require greater effort and time. But for most basic issues, it works well.

PUTTING IT INTO PRACTICE

Think of an issue in your home where limits are required to be designed or restated.

· What is the situation?
· How might gentle reminders encourage compliance?
· Write out a handful of gentle reminders you might need to use, and say them out loud. Practise them so when you need them, they are automatic.

There are dozens of additional strategies for effectively teaching our children. They may be as unique as each family, or even each individual within each family. Each of the principles and strategies given here for teaching good ways to act has a time and place. You understand your child and, as the expert on your family, you can discern which is appropriate and when.

Effective discipline is most likely to occur as we take the time to be emotionally available and really understand our children. This helps us to recognise and acknowledge our children's level of development, working with them rather than doing things to them. We can teach good ways to act through effective and repetitive induction (where we ask more questions rather than giving the answers), taking our child's perspective and encouraging them to take the perspective of others and using gentle reminders. As we do so, we increase the likelihood that their behaviour will be for the right reasons, rather than because we are 'making' them do as we have asked.

Notes

1 HW Goddard, *Soft-spoken parenting: 50 ways to not lose your temper with your kids*, Silverleaf Press, Seattle, 2007.
2 MB Rosenberg, *Nonviolent communication: a language of life*, 2nd edn, PuddleDancer Press, California, 2003, p. 165.
3 MA Straus & MJ Paschall, 'Corporal punishment by mothers and development of children's cognitive ability: A longitudinal study of two nationally representative age cohorts', *Journal of Aggression, Maltreatment & Trauma*, vol. 18, no. 5, 2009, pp. 459–483.
4 JC Coulson, LG Oades & GJ Stoyles, 'Parents' subjective sense of calling in childrearing: Measurement, development and initial findings', *The Journal of Positive Psychology*, vol. 7, no. 2, 2012, pp. 83–94.
5 CA Taylor, JA Manganello, SJ Lee & JC Rice, JC, 'Mothers' spanking of 3-year-old children and subsequent risk of children's aggressive behaviour', *Pediatrics*, vol. 125, no. 5, 2010, pp. 1057–65.
6 MA Straus & MJ Paschall, 2009.
7 T Dobbs & J Duncan, 'Children's perspectives on physical discipline: a New Zealand example', *Child Care in Practice*, vol. 10, no. 4, 2004, pp. 367–79.
8 A Kohn, *Beyond discipline: from compliance to communication*, 10th anniversary edn, Association for Supervision and Curriculum Development, Alexandria, Virginia, 2006, p. 24.
9 ET Gershoff, A Grogan-Kaylor, JE Lansford, L Chang, A Zelli, K Deater-Deckard & KA Dodge, 'Parent discipline practices in an international sample: associations with child behaviors and moderation by perceived normativeness', *Child Development*, vol. 81, no. 2, 2010, pp. 487–502.
10 DB Bugental & JE Grusec, 'Socialization processes', in N Eisenberg, W Damon & RM Lerner (eds), *Handbook of child psychology: Vol. 3, Social, emotional and personality development*, 6th edn, John Wiley & Sons, Hoboken, New Jersey, 2006, pp. 366–428.
JC Gibbs, *Moral development and reality: beyond the theories of Kohlberg and Hoffman*, 2nd edn, Penguin, New York, 2010.
EE Maccoby, 'The role of parents in the socialization of children: an historical overview', *Developmental Psychology*, vol. 28, no. 6, 1992, pp. 1006–17.
11 J Piaget, *The child's conception of the world*, Frogmore, St Albans, UK, 1973.
12 HW Goddard, 'Are children angels, devils or clay?', presentation at Family Expo conference, The University of Queensland, 2004.

Kindness, Compassion, Love

4

'What wisdom can you find that is greater than kindness?'
Jean-Jacques Rousseau[1]

This book is about having a happy family. But what is a happy family?

A popular 'mummy blogger' thought that she had everything covered. Her house was the kind of place you'd see in magazines. Her husband and two children offered her joy, opportunities to feel grateful and a sense of purpose. Her husband provided well. In spite of all this, it seems that one day it all got too much. Sleep deprivation, the challenges of raising her children through some of their more 'difficult' times and the expectation that families are supposed to be 'happy' combined to create a feeling of hopelessness and depression. Emily wrote:

> *Some days I do a great job of being a stay-at-home mum while other days I find doing endless loads of washing rather unfulfilling. For me, it's a day by day thing. Some days I cope, others I don't. Some days there is a hot dinner and a clean house, others there's not. Today is one of the 'other' days. No hot dinner, no happy children, not even any clean washing. But there have been tears and tantrums a plenty.[2]*

Emily's experience is not unique. Whatever your circumstances, if you are a parent, you have experienced precisely the same things. Parenting is tough. Some days are tougher than others. We have expectations of happy children and a happy home, and some days – or even most days – we simply cannot get there. We find ourselves asking, 'Is a consistently happy family a possibility?'

For the most part, we will not have very many completely happy days. In fact, there are vast quantities of research that show that having children is bad for your happiness. Study after study reveals that, in general, family life can be fitted to a U-shaped happiness curve. As couples procreate and bring offspring into their lives, their happiness goes down. Parents with children at home report being less satisfied with life, and experiencing fewer positive emotions than adults without children. One notable study found that mothers were significantly happier doing the laundry, cleaning, cooking, shopping or socialising than they were when they were spending time with their children.[3] Parents have higher levels of stress and worry, and are more anxious and depressed than those without children. It gets worse as our kids turn into teenagers. We experience sleep deprivation, extreme negotiations over everything from music and hairstyles to curfews and car privileges. It is not until our children gain their independence (and we regain ours) that our happiness rises back to pre-child levels. Most researchers agree that these outcomes are due to financial constraints, time pressures and the ongoing challenges of raising a child.[4] It doesn't have to be like this. By practising the strategies in this book, we can alleviate some of those decreases in wellbeing. Perhaps, though, looking for happiness means we are looking for the wrong things.

Happiness versus meaningfulness

Given that you have read this far into this book, you may have noticed something. The principles that are described rarely relate to being 'happy'. Instead, themes like meaningfulness, building and strengthening, sacrifice, patience and challenges are emphasised. They're not the kinds of things we normally think of when we think about being happy.

To reinforce my point, think carefully about the following exercise. It requires a good deal of reflection. It may help clarify your thoughts if there is someone you can talk with about your experiences.

Points to ponder

- What are the *happiest* moments you have had with your family? What was going on? How were you involved? What was everyone doing? Recreate your response with as much detail as possible. How were people acting towards one another? Why?
- What are the most *meaningful* moments you have had with your family? What was going on? How were you involved? What was everyone doing? Recreate your response with as much detail as possible. How were people acting towards one another? Why?

Compare your happy moments with your meaningful moments. What do you notice about the examples you have thought through?

Perhaps your happy moments involved special occasions with the whole family together. It may have been a family camping trip, a Christmas Day, a bar mitzvah. There may have been times when parents felt no pressure – when children were chatting over dinner, running around a park, swimming at the beach.

Now look at the meaningful moments you have experienced with your family. Perhaps there is some overlap between the lists, and you have identified those same times when you were completely present, basking in the feelings of happiness that come from being together. Or there may have been times when everyone was working together, contributing, helping. There may be meaningful moments that have come as you and your spouse have struggled through sleep deprivation, teething, tantrums or adolescent rebellion. Meaning may have come to your family through the difficulty of watching your child struggle socially at school, underperform academically or other challenges.

We want the happy moments. They are essential for family life so that we can flourish as families. But we need the difficult times as well. They help us recognise and appreciate the good times for what they are, and they help us develop and grow. It is something of a paradox, but our eventual levels of happiness are raised because we are willing to have them lowered through years of dirty nappies, tantrums and attitude. In other words, the difficult phases that we have been through become deeply meaningful to us as time passes. Given space, we reflect on those difficult times with a fresh perspective – one that fills us with satisfaction for being able to work through such challenges. And as we reflect on what our family has become because of those challenges, we feel happier. A willingness to be unhappy leads to meaning, purpose and fulfilment, which ultimately enhances our happiness.

Gleaning gold flecks from family life

In the mid-1800s there were significant gold rushes around the world. A well-known story tells of a young man who, like thousands of others, was certain that if he went to the goldfields he would find gold nuggets too big to carry and be set for life.

The man sold everything he had in order to make the journey, and when he arrived at the goldfields, he set to work. He dipped his pan into the river, washed the water over the sediments, and, over time, became more and more disappointed. He was persistent, but at no point did he find a gold nugget. Not even the smallest pebble.

As the days wore on, he accumulated a massive pile of rocks beside him. He would dip his pan, wash the sand and pebbles with water, remove the rocks, place them beside where he sat, and dip his pan back into the river. He was sure that if he persisted he would find the one nugget he needed to make the venture worthwhile.

Things became desperate for the young man. He was out of money, and still had no gold nuggets. He was approached by an older, wealthy prospector who commented on the size of the pile of rocks the young man had accumulated.

Dejectedly, the young man confirmed his fears to the prospector. 'I've been here for months looking for gold, but there isn't any. I'm going home.'

The old prospector disagreed. 'I wouldn't be so sure. You just have to know where to find it.' He then took two rocks from the young man's pile and smashed them together. One rock split, and gold flecks reflected the sunlight, sparkling in the older man's hand.

But the inexperienced young man had higher expectations. He wanted perfection. He wanted nuggets, not tiny flecks. He said that he wanted nuggets like the ones hanging from the pouch on the old man's belt.

The old man lifted his bulging pouch from his belt and held it out to the young man who took it, opened it up and peered inside. He was shocked. There was not one single nugget. Instead, the pouch was full of thousands of those tiny gold flecks.

The wise old prospector told the young man that he was looking for the wrong thing, explaining, 'You are chasing gold nuggets so hard that you're missing out on all the enormous wealth that these precious gold flecks can bring you. It's the slow, methodical, daily grind of accumulating these little gold flecks that has brought me the wealth I enjoy today.'

As parents, we often look for happiness in family life in the same way that the young merchant was looking for gold. We expect that family life is supposed to bring us big, joyful moments of happiness. We want the nuggets that will make us rich. We want to feel good. We want the magazine-family life!

But what if family life is not meant to be all about golden, happy moments? What if family life is about something entirely different?

Parenting is about parents, not children

Parenting is called 'parenting' because the process is less about our children and more about us, as adults. The flecks of gold in family life are often disguised as big, heavy rocks and it is up to us, as parents, to do the heavy lifting. Family life gives us a remarkable course in self-development. We learn to be patient, compassionate and charitable. We learn to serve. We sacrifice. When we do these things grudgingly, parenting is like panning for gold and getting nothing but those big, heavy rocks. We keep dipping into that dirty river that we have come to despise. We resent it. We see parenting as a job – a chore. We just have to keep going and maybe one day we'll find the gold.

When we learn patience, compassion, charity, service and sacrifice for our children and do these things willingly, something interesting happens. We see our role as parent as an opportunity for our own development and our children's development. Our focus is on being the best we can be for our children. And we become better people as a result. More than this, we do better as well.

My research has demonstrated that there is a powerful relationship between parents' feelings towards being a parent, and several important variables.[5] For example, compared to those who feel that being a parent is just another job, the more that we feel that our parenting role is a major purpose in our lives, the more likely it is that we will feel satisfied with our lives. We'll also experience more positive emotion than those who see the role as a job – so we'll be happier and more satisfied with life. Importantly, we'll derive significant meaning from being a parent, and we'll practise better parenting habits. Parents who have this optimal orientation are far more likely to do the kinds of things that are spoken of in this book (being emotionally available, taking time to understand, showing warmth and compassion as they teach good ways to act, setting appropriate limits and so on).

One of the most interesting findings from my research is that the children of parents with this optimal orientation to parenting do far better than the children of parents who see parenting as a chore. Adolescents' scores on positive emotion, life satisfaction and the degree to which they are engaged in life are each positively related to their parents' subjective sense that their role is what they are supposed to be doing with their life. As parents' scores on the importance of parenting go up, so do their children's scores on these important wellbeing characteristics.

But how do we make our attitude towards being a parent fit this ideal picture? The first thing we might consider is how we think about parenting. Simply put, do we see it as one of the most important things we can do? Or is it just another job that keeps getting in the way? Are we positive about parenting? Or do we see children as an impediment to an otherwise well-ordered life? The cognitive framing we put around parenting has an impact on the extent to which we gain happiness and meaning from family life. If we can construct a system of meaning – a greater purpose – around parenting, we may be more likely to feel a sense that parenting really matters.

After we consider the way we are thinking about parenting, we can consider the relationships that make up our parenting life. Changing the nature of our interactions with our children will almost certainly generate a fundamental shift in the way we feel about being a parent. Discovering ways to spend additional time together (perhaps on special 'dates' with a child for some quality one-on-one time, or playing games) can provide opportunities to change the way we perceive our role. We can practise improved relational habits. We can spend time with our children and see them as people, and not just 'the ones I'm always cleaning up after'. These kinds of changes help us to spend more time being emotionally available and understanding our children.

Third, we can change the things that we do as parents to make them fit better with family life. Parents who see their role as meaningful and something they want to do well at are more likely to schedule their work in such a way that it impacts less on time with their children, or on priorities related to parenting. Deciding to mow the grass and wash the car during the week so as to focus on and enjoy the time with children on the weekend provides a simple example of this kind of task-oriented change. Of course, some changes could be counter-productive. Skipping work consistently to attend every school assembly or sports event may create greater stress in other areas of life. Wisdom, prudence and balance are needed. Moreover, not all families will benefit from leaving the dishes in the sink until all children are in bed. For some families completing such tasks may intrude on meaningful moments, but for others, time at the kitchen sink may be an opportunity to bond together.

PUTTING IT INTO PRACTICE

Several of these ideas are the culmination of things that have been suggested in earlier parts of this book, but it is useful to revisit them here.

· Think about your role as a parent. Is your attitude a good one, or do you think of parenting as a chore? What specific things can you do to improve the way you think about being a parent?

· Think about the relationships you have created with your children. Do you actually make time for your relationships to be more than transactional? Or are you too busy to do more than give orders, provide meals, clean up and put your children to bed? What specific things can you do to re-craft the relationships you have with your children?

· Think about the tasks you do in relation to your parenting. Are you prioritising the right tasks at the right time? Are there things about the tasks you are doing that could be modified to help you be a more connected, involved, engaged parent?

None of these questions is easy to answer, or easy to put into practice. But by thinking about them, trying new things and emphasising the relationship you have with your children, you may find that your family can be happier.

Kindness makes families happiest

Every idea in this book can be distilled into a few key words aimed at making us better people so that we can be better parents: compassion, empathy, kindness, love. When we take the time to be emotionally available to our children, we exhibit these virtues. When we practise understanding, we practise these virtues and make them a habit. When we discipline with a desire to teach and guide rather than to punish, our emphasis is on compassion, empathy, kindness and love. It seems, then, that the best way to have a happy family is to be kind. Harold Koenig, in his book *Kindness and Joy*, says:

> *Kindness … is a gentle, caring form of love … and is often communicated with a soft touch, a warm embrace, a caring look, or an understanding smile … It can be very simple, like going out of one's way to be courteous, considerate, or nice to others … Real kindness is altruistic and generous at its core … Kindness expects nothing in return, and is wholly focussed on the other person's good.[6]*

Too often, with so much going on in our lives, and with the intimate familiarity that family life offers, kindness becomes one of the first neglected virtues. It's an incredibly simple principle, but it can be one of the most difficult virtues to enact. It is our responsibility, as parents, to consider the needs of our children, even when this requires us to look past our own personal needs. Kindness in our thoughts, words and deeds is a great challenge. Yet, when we experience it, kindness at home makes families happy. When our families work best, kindness underpins every interaction. It is a lofty ideal, and there will be days when we fail miserably. That is normal. But kindness is a foundation that we will do well to strive for in family life.

The following story illustrates how kindness can be the critical element that makes a family function, even under duress. As you read through this story, you will see how it incorporates all of the principles that have been discussed throughout the previous chapters. You will also note that the ability to be kind, compassionate and loving with our children is not a technique. It comes from a desire to be a great parent, and a willingness to put our lives on hold for our children because they are what matters most to us.

It was early afternoon when Mrs Blunzon's phone rang. She answered it and heard a voice say, 'Hello Mrs Blunzon, it's the school principal here. I'm calling because we've had a serious issue with your son, Fin. He has threatened another child in Grade One today, and it is quite severe. Will you please come to the school so that I can discuss it with you, and perhaps you can take Fin home?'

Once she arrived at the school, Mrs Blunzon was shown into the principal's office where her son, Fin, sat. He was staring at the floor when she walked in. He glanced up at her briefly but would not look at her after that.

The principal spoke politely but firmly. 'Are you familiar with the peanut allergy many children have? Are you aware that we have a ban on nuts at this school? Are you aware that a child with the allergy, Simon, is in your child's class?'

Mrs Blunzon responded, 'Yes', to each of the questions she was asked.

Then the principal told Mrs Blunzon, 'This morning, Fin brought peanuts to school, and shook them in Simon's face, screaming, "I'm going to kill you!"

Fin's mother was stunned. She was embarrassed. She was furious!

The principal suggested that Fin be taken home to work through the situation. He asked that Mrs Blunzon discuss the outcome with him and that Fin report back to her the following day to describe what had happened at home.

Imagine that you were this mother and answer the following questions in your mind:

• What would you say to Fin in the car on the way home?
• What would you do?
• Would your 'natural' responses to the situation be justified?
• Would they be helpful in terms of your son's development and your relationship with him?

During my workshops I share this real experience with parents and their responses are invariably the same. They assure me that while being emotionally available and understanding might be important, in this instance, they would have to revert back to the more 'standard' ways we parent in our society. They suggest that they would probably yell, threaten, ground their children, drive the car fast, yell some more and then extend the grounding period. Many of them admit that they would be so furious they would probably physically punish their children too. But would any of this be effective in teaching Fin? What would he learn?

Chances are that he might not learn much about good ways to act. He may learn that Mum and Dad are scary people when they're angry. He may become sneakier about doing things so Mum and Dad don't find out. He may also start to think that anyone in any position of authority (like the school or other people's parents) can also get him in trouble. It is less likely that he will learn to treat other people kindly.

How will he feel about himself, as a person, if we approach our 'discipline' in a more traditional, punitive way? He will probably feel that he is not a good person, that he is not worthy of goodness from others. He may feel that he is everything he is about to be called by his mum, or his teacher – that is, 'I am a stupid idiot. I am a brat. I am selfish and thoughtless'. If we go on and on at our children, regardless of how bad their actions are, it is unlikely that any real discipline will be carried out. They will certainly be punished, but lengthy time-outs or physical punishments will not teach. In this situation, these methods will give Fin plenty of reasons to consider why he hates his mum, or his teacher or Simon. But he will not think about how he can act more appropriately. He will not become a better person because of his punishment. In fact, he may even feel justified in what he has done, or look for ways to get even with those who are now hurting *him*.

Let's look at this scenario from a loving and compassionate viewpoint. Did Fin know that he was doing the wrong thing? Probably, yes. If he knew he had done the wrong thing, how would he have been feeling about it by the time he was sitting in the principal's office? I suspect he would have been scared – even if he had a good relationship with his mother.

> When Mrs Blunzon called me about the situation, I suggested that they have a quiet ride home. Perhaps she might hold his hand if he would let her, but he may not. I suggested that she explain to Fin that they both needed a little quiet time alone, so that they could think about what had happened during the day. After some time-out for mum, they might sit together.
>
> By making herself completely available and mindful, Mrs Blunzon is enacting the first key to a connected family, and is giving Fin precisely what he needs at this moment.

'He probably won't want to be near me', she replied.

I hinted that by making herself emotionally available, Fin may be responsive. 'You might show him that you understand how he is feeling. Perhaps saying something like "You're feeling pretty awful about things right now, aren't you?" might work. Tell him you know he has had a bad day. Then ask him if he'd like to talk about it, or just cuddle you. Chances are he'll probably cry a lot. He's pretty emotional at the moment.'

Six-year-olds might struggle to maintain composure in these circumstances. I asked Mrs Blunzon if she felt she could sit with him, hold him and listen to him share his feelings. She agreed that she could do that. I asked if she could quietly restate his feelings to show she understood. Again, Mrs Blunzon felt that this was achievable. We discussed how this process might take considerable time. If Fin was worked up he would need a lot of emotional availability and a lot of understanding.

It's always interesting when I teach this process in workshops. At least one parent will interrupt to argue that Fin doesn't need this soft stuff. What he really needs is a good kick up the bum! As tempting as it might be, such an approach will alienate Fin, and will stop him really learning. Conversely, unconditional love will allow Fin to calm down, soften and be open to being taught – or reminded – of good ways to act.

'Once Fin has calmed down, we need to teach him. That's the real discipline', I reminded Mrs Blunzon. I suggested that she let him know that she understood that he probably didn't really want to talk about what had happened.

'State the facts as you understand them, and then ask questions. But beyond that basic statement, as an introduction, it is important that you don't do the talking. When your mouth is moving, he is not learning. So ask him a soft question about the incident, using perspective taking. No interrogation about why he did it. Ask him, "How do you think Simon felt when you did what you did?"

'When you bring that up, Fin will probably start crying again', I suggested. 'He's only little and he is dealing with some big emotions. So hold him. Describe his emotions. And when he has calmed down, let him know you need to work out what he understands. Kindly ask him again, "How did Simon feel, do you think, when you shook the nuts at him and said you'd kill him?"'

At this point, we are beginning to effectively introduce perspective taking into our discipline. As Fin sees the perspective of Simon, he is far more likely to learn from this process. He has calmed down somewhat. He knows he is in a safe place to talk. He is able to share what he really feels.

'Over time, with your patience, Fin will be able to answer the question. Then it might be appropriate to have Fin think about what Simon dealt with the previous afternoon. He could describe what Simon talked with his parents about. All of these things give Fin an understanding of how Simon felt. And Fin's insights are where his learning occurs.'

Mrs Blunzon could see how some aspects of this might work for Fin. Then she asked me, 'But what about the consequences? Surely he should be punished'.

'Consequences and punishment are different', I explained. 'Punishment happens when you do something nasty to Fin to hurt him in some way, or make him suffer. To help Fin deal with the consequences of his actions, he needs to consider what those consequences are for Simon. We might also ask Fin what the consequences of his actions are on various other things, like his relationship with other people at school, his feelings about himself, and so on. His action has consequences, but we do not have to enforce extra ones on him. As he sees the consequences that his actions naturally have, he will learn. It's our job, as parents, to help him see.'

'Surely he has to say sorry, though', Mrs Blunzon stated.

'As a consequence of his behaviour, Fin has alienated himself from Simon', I said. 'If he wishes to reinstate his relationship with Simon, he will probably need to make some form of restitution. But we can't make him do it. He has to decide for himself.'

As it turned out, Fin did cry a lot. He was reluctant to talk to his parents. He was scared. Over the next couple of days, however, Fin went through the process outlined above with his mother. She asked him the right questions, once he felt safe, to develop answers that would lead to real learning and discipline:

'What did Simon feel when you did that?'

'How is Simon going to feel next time he sees you at school?'

'What do you suppose Simon is talking to his parents about this afternoon?'

'How is Simon's family going to feel about you, and about us?'

'What do you think needs to happen to make things better?'

Fin developed answers and solutions himself, while his mum sat beside him, listened, reflected emotions, offered gentle guidance and allowed him to determine the best course of action, which ultimately included an apology. He worked with his mother and his teacher and principal to restore a damaged relationship, based on ideas he developed with people who cared enough about him to be compassionate, kind and loving even when he seemed like he didn't deserve it.

By taking a compassionate approach to Fin, his mother learned more about him as well. It turned out that Fin was feeling overwhelmed by his parents' recent separation and pending divorce. He was struggling with the alienation he felt from his dad. He felt lost and powerless. He wanted some attention, some love. Because Fin's mum was able to work *with* him rather than doing things to him, the incident became a teaching moment – a time of growth and meaning, and something that brought a family closer together rather than becoming something that drove a wedge between a little boy and his mum. In many ways, an ugly 'boulder' became a series of 'flecks of gold'.

Our children most need our love, compassion and kindness when they are being the most unlovable. That's when they need to know that, even when they do the wrong thing, we are there for them. Loving unconditionally doesn't mean condoning our children's inappropriate behaviour. It doesn't mean we let them get away with things. But for teaching to be effective, our children need to feel understood and safe – they need to always feel loved.

The hardest part of being a parent

Parenting is harder than brain surgery or rocket science or rocket surgery! Our children challenge us constantly. They push boundaries; they hurt each other – and us. They refuse to listen. They make mess and don't clean it up. They wake us up early on Saturday mornings. These things make parenting challenging, but we will do well to remember that children find life challenging as well.

> My third daughter has experienced great difficulty with her speech and language. This has required us to employ a speech therapist to work with her for several years. We have seen remarkable success and great gains in all areas, for which we are thankful. Yet Ella is still not like other girls her age. Sure, she loves to dance and sing – and does so with absolute passion. But she still struggles to communicate, gets very frustrated in ways that most girls her age have grown out of and thinks a little differently to those at similar ages.
>
> One afternoon when Ella was seven, she sat with me in the car. As we drove she unexpectedly said to me, choking down a sob, 'Dad, I'm sad because I don't understand things like everyone else can understand them'.

Ella demonstrated remarkable insight into something that many people think, but few people say. In effect she was saying, 'I'm different, Dad. And I don't want to be different. I want to be like everyone else'.

The greatest challenge we face as parents is remembering that our children's struggles are real. In the busyness of juggling priorities and trying to be all things to all people we often forget this. We expect our children to toe the line, do as we ask and cooperate so the family can function; so we can be happy. But the world is a big, confusing, difficult place for many – if not most – children. Our children need us to stop. They need us to feel with them. They struggle with our judgements, punishments and criticisms. They flourish with our patient, compassionate, kind, loving guidance. Our unconditional love gives them reassurance, security and a healthy confidence to explore the world. They can feel valued despite their shortcomings. They can feel loved.

As parents, we cannot always make things 'all better' for our children. In fact, recent research suggests that our children need to have struggles in order to develop grit, determination and a will to succeed.[7] It seems that struggling, failing and trying again can be something that makes our children stronger. But our availability, understanding and support contribute to their resilience and their positive development.

Parenting is about priorities: What are yours?

Making changes

When I run my parenting training sessions, I like to conclude with an activity where I invite each participant to stand up and turn to the person next to them. They are to carefully observe what their partner looks like, and then turn so that they are back-to-back. When they have done this, I ask them to change three things about their appearance. This is sometimes met with grumbles or snickering. The partners then turn back to face one another and are asked to identify the changes that have been made. They generally feel pretty successful and complete this task quite comfortably. Then I ask them to return to their position, back-to-back, and change a further three things. There are more grumbles than chuckles this time. The activity is harder. Changing three things is not particularly tough, but some people lack sufficient clothing to change much more! By this stage people find it more difficult to isolate what the new changes to appearance were. After some time to work out the answers, I ask participants to stand back-to-back again, and change another three things. While one or two people begin, most of the audience groans. It is generally at this point that I ask everyone to resume their seats and we discuss the activity.

What does this teach us about change?

1 We all have a different capacity for change. Some people find it very easy to change many, many things about themselves, while others struggle.
2 We all have a different approach to change, and different levels of willingness to be involved in change. While many people enjoy the opportunity to do something different, there are lots of people who resent being asked to think, or being challenged.
3 Even for those with a large capacity for change, and a willingness to change, change can be difficult and require work.
4 We make the easiest changes that provide least resistance first.
5 When changes are made, some are subtle and some are glaring.
6 We make changes based on others' opinions. With very few exceptions, people make sure that any changes they are making are kept within the social norms of our society.

Perhaps the most important point of the workshop exercise, however, occurs when our discussion is all but over. As we conclude our conversation about change, I casually ask everyone, 'How many of you have changed back to what you were comfortable with?' In every case, without exception, every single person in the room has uncreased their clothing, put their earrings back in, replaced their shoes, pulled their socks up or down, repositioned their glasses, and returned, one hundred per cent, to the way they had been before the change exercise began.

When we make changes, regardless of what we are making changes for, we find it particularly difficult to maintain them. Within a few weeks, we generally return to our default position. Sometimes this is a good thing. Some of the changes we wish to make are not good ones for us. More often than not, however, our attempts at change come unstuck due to a lack of resolve or force of habit. We are attempting to make important, positive changes that can make a difference to us and to those around us. Yet we struggle to achieve the change we seek and we go back to the way we were.

As you consider the things you have read within the pages of this book, you will have been reminded of many things you already know. You may have read several things you had not thought of before. Hopefully, there are a few things that have resonated with you and motivated you to want to make some changes to improve your family. The great challenge now is to make those changes last. Remember that some things you try – even with the best of intentions – may not work at all, and could make things worse. These things may be different for each person and each family. As parents, we all have different ways of living and being, different temperaments, schedules, priorities and thought processes. The ideas discussed in this book are generally right for most people most of the time, but they may not all work every time for every person. Further to this, each child is different. Personalities and temperaments lend themselves to certain ways of doing things. So try things for a while and celebrate your victories. But also be willing to recognise that some of the things you try may not work for you and your family in your circumstances.

Notes

1   J-J Rousseau, *Émile ou De l'éducation* (Emile: Or, on education), 1762.
2   The Beetle Shack, 'Stay at home mumming and postnatal depression', 31 August 2011, <http://thebeetleshack.blogspot.com.au/2011/08/stay-at-home-mumming-and-postnatal. html>.
3   D Kahnemann, AB Krueger, DA Schkade, N Schwarz & AA Stone, 'A survey method for characterizing daily life experience: the day reconstruction method', *Science*, vol. 306, no. 5702, 2004, pp. 1776–80.
4   L Angeles, 'Children and life satisfaction', *Journal of Happiness Studies*, vol. 11, no. 4, 2010, pp. 523–38.
    S McLanahan & J Adams, 'Parenthood and psychological well-being', *Annual Review of Sociology*, vol. 13, 1987, pp. 237–57.
5   JC Coulson, LG Oades & GJ Stoyles, 'Parents' subjective sense of calling in childrearing: measurement, development and initial findings', *The Journal of Positive Psychology*, vol. 7, no. 2, 2012, pp. 83–94.
6   H Koenig, *Kindness and joy: expressing the gentle love*, Templeton Foundation Press, Philadelphia, 2006.
7   AL Duckworth, C Peterson, MD Matthews & DR Kelly, 'Grit: perseverance and passion for long term goals', *Journal of Personality and Social Psychology*, vol. 92, no. 6, 2007, pp. 1087–101.

Conclusion

Some years ago, my wife, Kylie, and I were running quite late for an event that was important to us. Kylie had not put her make-up on, and so as I drove, she flipped down the sun visor in front of the passenger seat and used the mirror to apply her make-up. In spite of the time pressure, and the knowledge that I would get into trouble for it, I could not help but hit a few bumps in the road.

I got the reaction I wanted and chuckled as I feigned an apology. However, there were also some bumps that were unavoidable. They crossed the entire road and nothing I could do could prevent us from hitting them. And there were occasional bumps that came upon us unexpectedly. Either a failure to observe the condition of the road, or a bend, glaring sunlight or another factor led to me hitting some bumps entirely by accident.

Family life is certain to contain many bumps. There are some bumps we go looking for, thinking it may be fun to hit them and watch the reactions. Teasing family members is an example of this. Sometimes it doesn't matter so much. Other times, careless teasing can lead to lifelong scarring and bitterness.

There are the bumps in the road that are unavoidable, such as toddler tantrums and teething, sleep deprivation, worry over children's schooling or rebellious teenage moods. Every parent experiences these kinds of bumps.

And there are the unexpected bumps – cyber-bullying, an accidentally broken window, a car accident with a learner driver.

As you seek happiness in your family, expect bumps in the road. They are inevitable. This book offers suggestions for effective ways to manage those bumps. By dealing with challenges in positive ways, even the bumps can become eventual sources of happiness and meaning in life.

Further Reading

Faber, A & Mazlish, E, 2012, *How to talk so kids will listen and listen so kids will talk*, 30th anniversary edn, Scribner, New York.

Ginnott, H, Ginott, A & Goddard, HW, 2003, *Between parent and child: the bestselling classic that revolutionized parent–child communication*, revised and updated, Three Rivers Press, New York.

Goddard, HW, 2007, *Soft-spoken parenting: 50 ways to not lose your temper with your kids*, Silverleaf Press, Seattle.

Gottman, J & DeClaire, J, 1998, *Raising an emotionally intelligent child*, Simon & Schuster, New York.

Kohn, A, 2005, *Unconditional parenting: moving from rewards and punishments to love and reason*, Atria Books, New York.

Porter, L, 2005, *Children are people too: a parent's guide to young children's behaviour*, 4th edn, East Street Communications, South Australia.

What Your Child Needs From You

Creating a connected family

Justin Coulson, PhD

Audio versions

Read by Justin Coulson, the audio versions of **What Your Child Needs From You** are the perfect solution for busy parents who find it difficult to sit and read a book undisturbed.

Available in CD and MP3 formats.

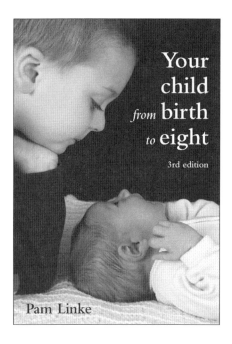

Your Child from Birth to Eight

3rd Edition

Pam Linke

Your Child from Birth to Eight provides a practical guide to the physical, emotional, social and cognitive development of young children, with a focus on fostering the bond between parent and child. While children develop differently in accordance with their genetic inheritance and environment, Pam Linke, renowned social worker and early childhood expert, clearly defines the steps which help parents to know what milestones children can be expected to reach, at different ages and stages and how best to support their learning.

In addition to developmental guidelines, **Your Child from Birth to Eight** offers ideas about suitable activities and toys for children as they grow. Tips and advice on issues to do with behaviour, emotions, temperament, toilet training, new siblings, sexual development and starting school are conveyed in an accessible and supportive style.

This fully revised and updated edition draws on contemporary research and provides insights into what is happening to children and why they may do what they do. An invaluable resource for all parents and carers, **Your Child from Birth to Eight** encapsulates the wisdom and experience of other mums and dads, as well as social workers, health professionals, early childhood practitioners and teachers who engage regularly with children aged from birth to eight.

About the author

Pam Linke AM is a social worker with a specific interest in early childhood. She is the author of many books and articles on young children and parenting. In 2006, Pam was awarded the Order of Australia for her professional services in the field.

sales@acer.edu.au | 03 9277 5447 | Order online: http://shop.acer.edu.au

www.acer.edu.au/publications/parenting

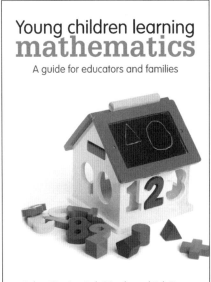

Young children learning
mathematics
A guide for educators and families

Robert Hunting, Judy Mousley and Bob Perry

Young Children Learning Mathematics

A guide for educators and families

Robert Hunting, Judy Mousley and Bob Perry

Can young children learn mathematics before school? What ideas and concepts are they capable of learning? How can adults develop a child's mathematical thinking from birth to five years?

Early learning plays a critical role in laying a foundation for later success in schooling. **Young Children Learning Mathematics: A guide for educators and families** explores the possibilities and potential for early childhood educators, parents and carers to stimulate young children's mathematical thinking. Drawing on the authors' significant research, it answers frequently asked questions about early childhood mathematics, discusses the experiences, activities and conversations that could lead to mathematics learning, and provides simple, easy-to-follow guidelines on introducing and building on the mathematical concepts underpinning play and activity in young children aged from birth to five.

About the authors

Robert Hunting is a Senior Lecturer in Mathematics Education at La Trobe University. His research interests include early mathematics learning, rational number learning, teaching experiment methodologies, teacher education and curriculum issues in mathematics education.

Judy Mousley is Associate Professor at Deakin University. She has been involved in mathematics education research and teaching at Deakin University for 30 years.

Bob Perry is Professor of Education at Charles Sturt University. His research interests include powerful mathematics ideas in preschool and the first years of school, educational transitions and preschool education in remote Indigenous communities.

sales@acer.edu.au | 03 9277 5447 | Order online: http://shop.acer.edu.au

www.acer.edu.au/publications/parenting